M000248594

NATIONAL GEOGRAPHIC
Reach

Language • Literacy • Content

Program Authors

Nancy Frey

Lada Kratky

Nonie K. Lesaux

Sylvia Linan-Thompson

Deborah J. Short

Jennifer D. Turner

NATIONAL GEOGRAPHIC LEARNING | CENGAGE Learning

wers

Literatu ace Lin, Jonda C. McNair, Anastasia Suen

Carmen A

acher Reviewers

Grad as

Krist *Teacher*
Lead rill Elementary School
Do L

Ciani
Teacher
291X
Bronx, NY

Jonathan Eversoll
International Baccalaureate
Curriculum Coach
Park Center Senior High
Brooklyn Park, MN

Barbara A. Genovese-Fraracci
District Program Specialist
Hacienda La Puente Unified School District
Hacienda Heights, CA

Vanessa Gonzalez
ESL Teacher/ESL Specialist
Rhoads Elementary
Katy, TX

Leonila Izaguirre
Bilingual-ESL Director
Pharr – San Juan – Alamo Independent
School District
Pharr, TX

Myra Junyk
Literacy Consultant
Toronto, ON, Canada

Susan Mayberger
Coordinator of ESL, Migrant and
Refugee Education
Omaha Public Schools
Omaha, NE

Stephanie Savage Cantu
Bilingual Teacher
Stonewall Jackson Elementary School
Dallas, TX

Annette Torres Elias
Consultant
Plano, TX

Sonia James Upton
ELL Consultant, Title III
Kentucky Department of Education
Frankfort, KY

NATIONAL GEOGRAPHIC LEARNING | CENGAGE Learning

Acknowledgments
Grateful acknowledgment is given to the authors, artists, photographers, museums, publishers, and agents for permission to reprint copyrighted material. Every effort has been made to secure the appropriate permission. If any omissions have been made or if corrections are required, please contact the Publisher.

Illustrator Credits:
Front Cover: Joel Sotelo

Acknowledgments and credits continue on page 295.

Copyright © 2017 National Geographic Learning, Cengage Learning

ALL RIGHTS RESERVED. No part of this work covered by the copyright herein may be reproduced, transmitted, stored, or used in any form or by any means graphic, electronic, or mechanical, including but not limited to photocopying, recording, scanning, digitizing, taping, web distribution, information networks, or information storage and retrieval systems, except as permitted under Section 107 or 108 of the 1976 United States Copyright Act, without the prior written permission of the publisher.

National Geographic and the Yellow Border are registered trademarks of the National Geographic Society.

For product information and technology assistance, contact us at
Customer & Sales Support, 888-915-3276

For permission to use material from this text or product, submit all requests online at **www.cengage.com/permissions**
Further permissions questions can be emailed to
permissionrequest@cengage.com

National Geographic Learning | Cengage Learning
1 Lower Ragsdale Drive
Building 1, Suite 200
Monterey, CA 93940

Cengage Learning is a leading provider of customized learning solutions with office locations around the globe, including Singapore, the United Kingdom, Australia, Mexico, Brazil, and Japan. Locate your local office at **www.cengage.com/global**.

Cengage Learning products are represented in Canada by Nelson Education, Ltd.

Visit National Geographic Learning online at **NGL.Cengage.com**
Visit our corporate website at **www.cengage.com**

Printed in the USA.
RR Donnelley, Willard, OH, USA

ISBN: 978-13054-93001
ISBN (CA): 978-13054-94558

Printed in the United States of America
15 16 17 18 19 20 21 22 23 24
13 12 11 10 9 8 7 6 5 4 3 2 1

Contents at a Glance

Table of Contents

Creature Features

(?) **BIG QUESTION**

How are animals different?

Read More

 = Comprehension Coach    = Interactive Whiteboard    = NGReach.com

Unit 5

SOCIAL STUDIES
▸ **Animal Features**
▸ **Animal Movement**

Skills

Categorize
Details

Make
Connections

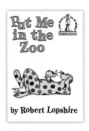

Table of Contents

Up in the Air

? **BIG QUESTION**
What's wild about weather?

Read More

 = Comprehension Coach  = Interactive Whiteboard  = NGReach.com

vi

Unit 6

SOCIAL STUDIES
▸ **Weather**
▸ **Seasons**

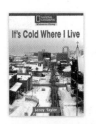

Table of Contents

Then and Now

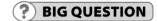
? BIG QUESTION

What's the difference
between then and now?

Read More

 = Comprehension Coach  = Interactive Whiteboard  = NGReach.com

SOCIAL STUDIES

▸ Past and Present
▸ Inventions and Technology

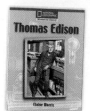

Table of Contents

Get Out the Map!

? BIG QUESTION
Why do we need maps?

Read More

 = Comprehension Coach 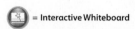 = Interactive Whiteboard  = NGReach.com

SOCIAL STUDIES
▸ **Maps**
▸ **Signs and Symbols**

Genres at a Glance

Nonfiction

Media

 = Interactive Whiteboard   = NGReach.com

Creature Features

?

BIG
Question

How are
animals
different?

Unit at a Glance
▶ **Language**: Compare and Contrast, Give Information, Science Words
▶ **Literacy**: Make Connections
▶ **Content**: Animals

Unit
5

Share What You Know

Do It!

1. **Draw** an animal.

2. **Name** or point to different parts of your animal.

3. **Say** or show how your animal moves.

Build background: Watch a video about animals.
NGReach.com

High Frequency
Words

and

but

too

Compare and Contrast

Listen and chant.

Legs

Chant (((MP3)))

Flamingos have legs,

And alligators do, **too**.

Alligators have four legs,

But flamingos have two!

leg

leg

4

Key Words

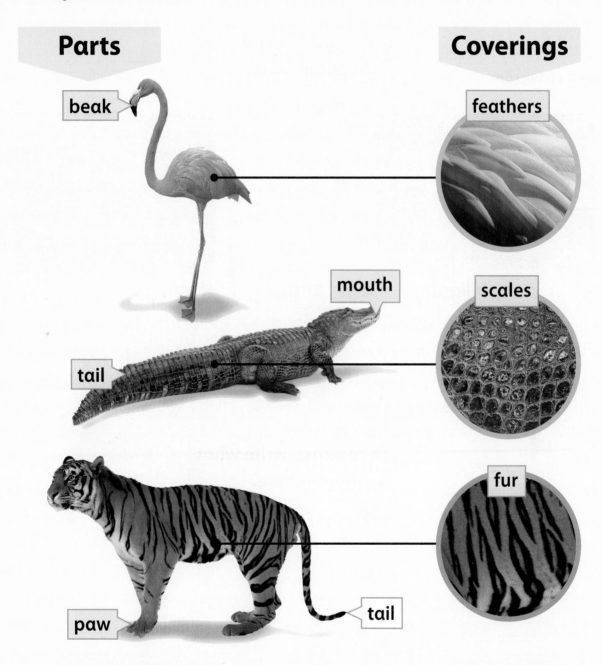

Parts

Coverings

beak

feathers

mouth

scales

tail

paw

tail

fur

Talk Together

Look at the parts and coverings of animals on this page. How are they different?

Compare and Contrast

Venn Diagram

To compare, write what is the same here.

alligator
- scales
- tail

both
- legs

flamingo
- feathers
- beak

To contrast, write what is different here.

Talk Together

Choose two animal picture cards. Make a Venn diagram. Compare and contrast the animals.

More Key Words

alike

These cats are **alike**.

• body

A baby has a small **body**.

different

These fruits are **different**.

feature

neck

A long neck is the main **feature** of a giraffe.

• look

These apples **look** the same.

Talk Together

Use one **Key Word** in a sentence.

I look like my brother.

• High Frequency Word

Add words to My Vocabulary Notebook.
NGReach.com

Read a Story

An **animal fantasy** is a story that is not true. The animals act like people.

Characters

Characters are the people or animals in the story.

Pete

Pete's Friends

Reading Strategy

Make connections as you read.
How are your feelings like Pete's feelings?

For Pete's Sake

by **Ellen Stoll Walsh**

Comprehension Coach

"I'm green," said Pete. "I want to be pink. Everyone else is."

"Don't worry," said the others. "You probably aren't ripe yet. It takes longer for some."

"Is that true?" Pete wondered.

"Probably," they said. "Let's play in the sand!"

"Oh no," cried Pete. "I have four feet.
No one else has four feet."

"You're lucky, Pete," said the others.
"Two, and two extra. C'mon. Let's
go wading."

Pete tried to feel lucky.
Before long he was having fun.

"Stop!" said the others, laughing.
"You're getting our **feathers** wet."
Uh-oh. Pete didn't have any feathers.

"The best feathers take the longest to grow," they said. "Hurry, it's getting late."

The others hurried home.

But poor, green, featherless Pete poked along on his four feet…

very, very slowly.

Nothing could cheer him up.

Then one day some strangers
stopped by on their way to the swamp.
Flamingos who **looked** just like Pete.
Pete almost popped with joy.

"I'm **different** but the same,"
he told the others.

"Well, for Pete's sake, Pete,"
they said. "You always have been." ❖

Meet the Author
Ellen Stoll Walsh

AWARD WINNER

Ellen Stoll Walsh has nine brothers and sisters. Ellen was the family storyteller.

Ellen grew up and started writing stories to read to her children. Now she can't imagine doing anything else!

Writer's Craft

Find words that Ellen Stoll Walsh used to show what Pete and his friends look like. Can you add some words?

Talk About It

1. What do Pete and his friends do together?

Pete and his friends ____ .

2. What does Pete want? Why?

Pete wants ____ . He ____ .

3. How can you tell that Pete's friends like him the way he is? Explain.

I can tell because Pete's friends ____ .

Learn test-taking strategies.
NGReach.com

Write About It

Make connections. How are your friends like Pete's friends? How are they **different**?

Pete's friends ____ and my friends are ____ .
Pete's friends ____ but my friends are ____ .

Compare Characters

How are the characters different?
How are they **alike**?

Venn Diagram

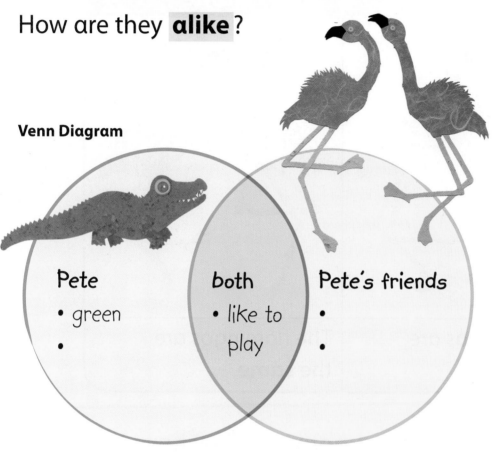

Pete
• green
•

both
• like to play

Pete's friends
•
•

Use your diagram. Tell a partner about Pete and Pete's friends.

Pete's friends have feathers.

31

Synonyms

alike	same

The flamingos are **alike**.	The flamingos are the **same**.

Alike and **same** are **synonyms**. They have the same meaning.

Try It Together

Talk about these pairs of words. Are they synonyms? Why or why not?

object	thing
sick	happy
bad	paw
quickly	fast

Connect Across Texts Learn more about what makes alligators **different**.

Genre A **science article** is nonfiction. This article gives information about alligators.

ALLIGATORS

by Julie Larson

An Alligator Home

Many alligators live in the Florida Everglades. The Everglades has many rivers and islands.

FLORIDA

The Everglades

Tallahassee ✪
Jacksonville
FLORIDA
Gulf of Mexico
Tampa
Miami
EVERGLADES

How do alligators' **bodies** help them live in the Everglades? Let's find out.

Alligator Bodies

Alligators have short legs. They can hide in tall grass. They can also hide under the water. Sometimes, you can only see their eyes. Can you see the alligator?

tail

Alligator Tails

Alligator **tails** can be more than 5 feet long. This is probably taller than you! Tails help alligators swim and move through the mud.

leg

Tails help alligators leap up to catch food.
Alligators can leap 5 feet into the air!

Compare Genres

How are *For Pete's Sake* and "Alligators" different?

Animal Fantasy

Then one day some strangers stopped by on their way to the swamp. Flamingos who **looked** just like Pete. Pete almost popped with joy.

Animals have feelings.

26

Science Article

Alligator Bodies
Alligators have short legs. They can hide in tall grass. They can also hide under the water. Sometimes, you can only see their eyes. Can you see the alligator?

gives information

Talk Together

Think about what you read and learned. How are animals different?

Complete Sentences

A **sentence** tells a complete thought.

An alligator's tail < **Not a sentence**

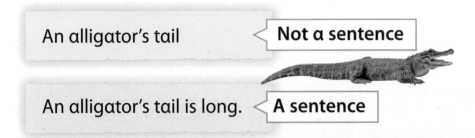

An alligator's tail is long. < **A sentence**

Grammar Rules Complete Sentences

	Complete Sentence
• Start with a **capital letter**. • End with an **end mark**, like a period. .	**capital letter** **A**lligator tails can be 10 feet long. **period**

Read a Sentence

Which group of words is a sentence?
How do you know?

1. leap up
2. Tails help alligators leap up to catch food.

Write a Sentence

Write a sentence about alligators. Read it to a partner.

Give Information

Listen and chant.

Chant ((MP3))

How Do They Move?

Animals move.
Yes, they do.
How do they go?
Do you know?

This is a fish.
A fish swims.
A fish uses fins to
move in water!

Fish swim.
Yes, they do.
How do they go?
Now you know!

Key Words

How do animals move?

swim

A fish swims.

fly

A bird flies.

run

A polar bear runs.

climb

A monkey climbs.

slide

A penguin slides.

slither

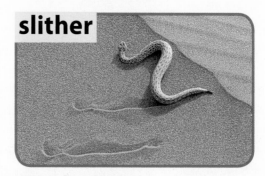

A snake slithers.

Talk Together

Act out how animals move. How are animals different?

Categorize Details

Category Chart

Animals	Movement
fish turtle	swim
	fly
	run

Write the big ideas here.

Write the details here.

Talk Together

Sort picture cards. Add animals to the Category Chart. Act out how the animals move. How are they different?

More Key Words

• back

The **back** tire is flat.

fact

It's a **fact** that a dog has four legs.

front

The **front** of the house is blue.

movement

The **movement** of a turtle is slow.

push

We had to **push** the car.

Talk Together

Use a **Key Word** to ask a question about animals.

What is one <u>fact</u> about turtles?

• High Frequency Word

Add words to My Vocabulary Notebook.
NGReach.com

Read a Fact Book

A **fact book** is nonfiction. It gives facts about things that are real.

✓ Look for labels.

feathers

wing

Reading Strategy

Make connections as you read. Connect new facts to things you have read in other texts and to things you know about the world.

Slither, Slide, Hop, and Run

by Katharine Kenah

Comprehension Coach

Fly

feathers

wing

A bird can **fly**! It moves through the air with wings.

Slither

A snake can **slither**! It wiggles from side to side on the ground.

Hop

back feet

A kangaroo can hop! It makes short leaps into the air. It uses its **back** feet to hop.

Run

leg

A horse can **run**! Its legs move forward
and backward very quickly.

Slide

hard shell

soft body

A snail can **slide**! It moves slowly along the ground. A snail has a soft body inside its hard shell.

Crawl

leg

A spider can crawl! It creeps forward
with its legs.

Hang

claws

A sloth can hang! It holds onto a tree
and hangs below it. A sloth has long claws.

Swim

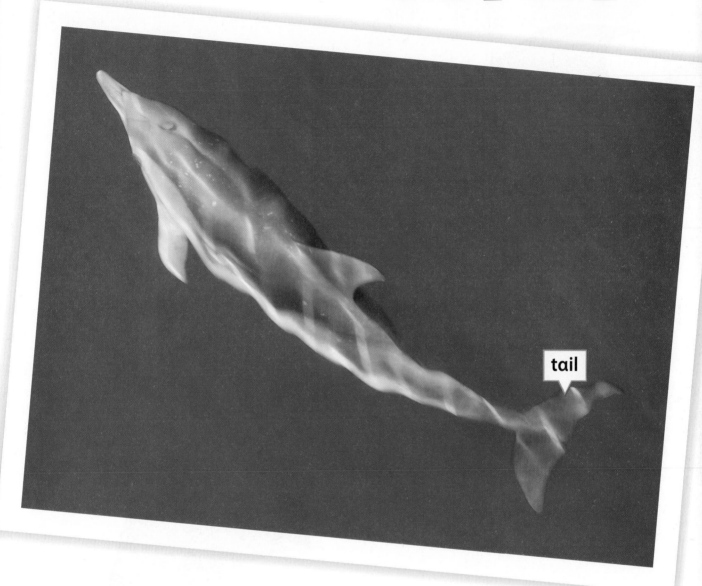

tail

A dolphin can **swim**! It moves gently through the water. A dolphin swims by moving its tail up and down.

Glide

wing

A bat can glide! It flies smoothly through the air. A bat's wings are really long fingers covered with skin.

Dig

paw

A dog can dig! It uses its paws to move dirt.

Climb

front foot

back foot

A raccoon can **climb**! It moves up and down by using its feet. Its **front** and back feet work like hands.

Waddle

A penguin can waddle! It rocks from side to side as it walks. A penguin can waddle as fast as a person walks!

Talk About It

1. What does the **fact** book tell you about animals?

The fact book tells ____ .

2. Name two animals in the book that slide on the ground.

____ and ____ slide on the ground.

3. How do other books you have read help you understand this fact book?

Other books help me ____ .

Learn test-taking strategies.
🖉 **NGReach.com**

Write About It

What is interesting about how animals move?
Write one sentence.

It is interesting that ____ .

Categorize Details

How do animals move?

Category Chart

Animals	Movement
birds bats	fly
horses	

Use your chart to summarize what you learned in *Slither, Slide, Hop, and Run.*

Antonyms

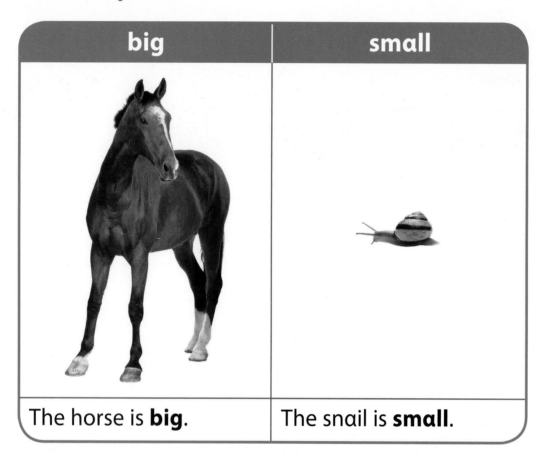

big	small
The horse is **big**.	The snail is **small**.

Big and **small** have opposite meanings. Words with opposite meanings are called **antonyms**.

Try It Together

Choose animal picture cards. Use the antonyms to compare the animals.

Antonyms	
big	small
fast	slow
front	back
hard	soft

NATIONAL
GEOGRAPHIC
EXCLUSIVE

Connect Across Texts Read about a camera that films animals moving in different ways.

Genre A **photo journal** shows something important in a person's life. It uses words and photos.

My Crittercam Journal

by Greg Marshall

July 8

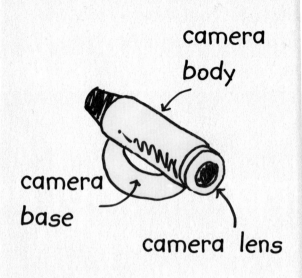

camera body

camera base

camera lens

Here's the camera my team and I made.
I call it Crittercam.

July 10

Today we put Crittercam on a whale.
I saw how it eats and swims.

August 20

I'm in Africa! Today Crittercam filmed a lion's movements. It runs fast!

August 21

Today I watched my Crittercam videos. The penguin video was really exciting.

Compare Genres

How are *Slither, Slide, Hop, and Run* and "My Crittercam Journal" alike and different?

Fact Book

Photo Journal

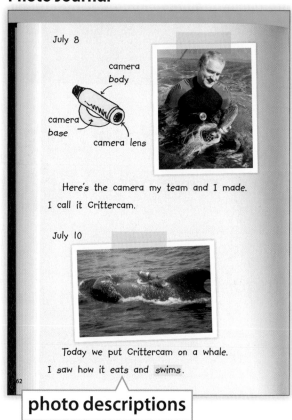

Talk Together

Think about what you read and learned. How are animals different?

Subject-Verb Agreement

In a sentence, the **subject** and the **verb**
go together.

One **frog** **hops**.

Two **frogs** **hop**.

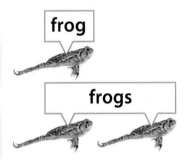

frog

frogs

Grammar Rules Subject-Verb Agreement

	Subject-Verb Agreement
If the **subject** names one, use **s** at the end of the **verb**.	If the **subject** names more than one, do not use **s** at the end of the **verb**.

Read a Sentence

Why does the verb below have **s**?

A dolphin **swims** in the ocean.

Write a Sentence

Write a sentence about how an animal moves.
Read it to a partner.

Write Like a Scientist

Write an Article ✏️

What do you know about animals? Describe an animal. Write an article for your classmates.

> ### Penguins
>
> by Roberto Garcia
>
> main idea ▷ **A penguin is a special bird**. Most birds have wings. Most birds use their wings to fly.
>
> details ▷ **A penguin has wings. But it doesn't fly**! Penguins use their wings to swim under water.
>
>

An article gives information about a topic.

❶ Plan and Write

Talk about animals with a partner. Pick an animal. Discuss your plan. Draw your animal and write a list of details. Tell your partner your main idea.

Write your main idea. Then write sentences with details.

❷ Check Your Work

Revise and edit your writing. Use this checklist.

Checklist
☑ Think about different words you can use. Can you use synonyms?
☑ Check your sentences. Did you use the right end mark?
☑ Trade work with a partner. Check the spelling. Correct spelling errors.

❸ Finish and Share

Finish your drawing. Write each sentence neatly. Make sure you leave enough space between each sentence.

Read your article aloud. Listen to your partner's article. Share what you know.

I know that peguins can't fly.

Share Your Ideas

Think about how animals move and look. How are animals different? Choose one of these ways to share your ideas about the **Big Question**.

Write It!

Draw and Label
Draw your favorite animal from the unit. Label the animal's parts. Write a sentence about your animal.

tail

legs   teeth

Alligators have four legs.

Talk About It!

Interview

Have an interview with a partner. The **reporter** asks questions about how animals look and move. The **expert** answers the questions.

How do penguins move?

They waddle!

Reporter

Expert

Do It!

I Am an Animal

Pretend you are an animal. Make a mask. In a group, act out how your animal moves.

Up in the Air

? BIG Question

What's wild about weather?

Unit at a Glance
▶ **Language:** Explain, Express Ideas, Science Words
▶ **Literacy:** Make Inferences
▶ **Content:** Weather

Unit
6

Share What You Know

Do It!

❶ **Name** your favorite kind of weather.

❷ **Tell** why you like that weather.

❸ **Draw** something you do in that weather.

Build Background: Watch a video about weather.
⟳ **NGReach.com**

Explain

Listen and sing.

Song

High Frequency
Words
can
how
made

Wind

The wind is made of air.

The wind is made of air.

Let me explain it one more time

How wind is made of air.

Wind can blow trees down.

And blow your hat around.

Let me explain it one more time

How wind can blow trees down.

Tune: "The Farmer in the Dell"

Key Words

What happens when the **wind** **blows**?

storm

Weather changes.

It can make electricity.

Things move.

It **feels** good.

Talk Together

Look at the windy weather. Explain what different kinds of wind can do. What is wild about wind?

Find Cause and Effect

Cause-and-Effect Chart

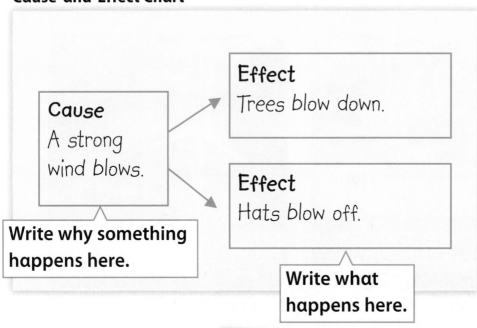

Cause	
Cause A strong wind blows.	**Effect** Trees blow down.
	Effect Hats blow off.

Write why something happens here.

Write what happens here.

Talk Together

Talk to a partner about rain. Explain what happens when it rains. Make a cause-and-effect chart.

More Key Words

fast

This car drives **fast**.

outside

They walk **outside**.

power

This toaster uses **power**.

soft

pillow

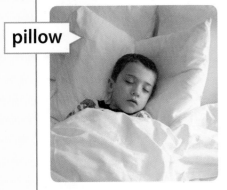

Pillows are **soft**.

strong

We are **strong**.

• High Frequency Word

Talk Together

Sort the **Key Words** by syllables.

One syllable fast

Two syllables outside

Add words to My Vocabulary Notebook.
NGReach.com

Read Science Nonfiction

Science nonfiction gives information about a science topic, like weather.

✓ Look for illustrations. Illustrations are drawings that show information.

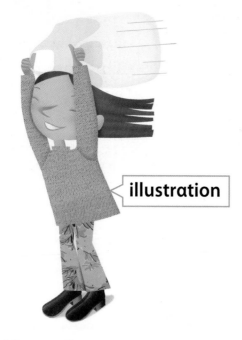

illustration

Reading Strategy

Make inferences as you read. Use what you know and details from the text to make inferences about what wind does.

I Face the Wind

by **Vicki Cobb**

illustrated by **Julia Gorton**

Comprehension Coach

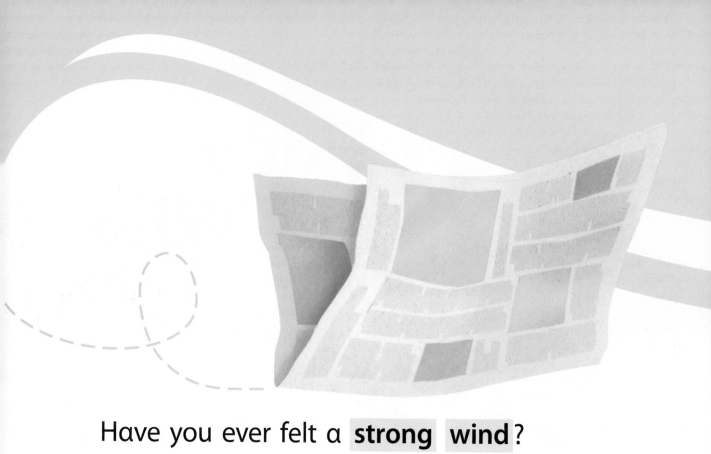

Have you ever felt a **strong** **wind**?

Your hair **blows** away from your face. You could lose your hat. You may even have to walk at a slant.

You can't see the wind. But you can **feel** it. And you can see what wind does to other things.

It makes flags stick out straight and flutter.

Can you name some things you see wind do?

Go **outside** and watch.

Leaves on trees shake.

A kite stays in the sky.

An umbrella turns inside out.

What is wind made of?

Wind is made of air. You can't see air. But you can catch it. Here's how:

1 Open a large plastic bag.

Make sure there are no holes in it.

2 Pull the bag through the air so it puffs up.

3 Twist it closed to trap the air you caught.

4 Squeeze the bag to feel the air.

Are there other ways you can make wind?

Blow air out of your mouth. Wave your hand in front of your face. Be an inventor and make your own kind of air movers.

The **fastest** winds of all are in a tornado. These winds are so strong they can lift a roof right off a house!

One of the **softest** winds is your
breath. Put your fingertips near your
nose. Feel your soft breath.

Face the wind. Feel the push of the wind. Yay! ❖

Talk About It

1. What is **wind** made of?

Wind is made of _____ .

2. What happens when the wind **blows**?

When the wind blows, _____ will _____ .

3. Why might you have to walk at a slant when a **strong** wind blows?

You might have to walk at a slant because _____ .

Learn test-taking strategies.
🅖 NGReach.com

Write About It ✏️

Use the illustrations and steps on pages 86 and 87. Retell how to catch air.

You can catch air _____ .

Find Cause and Effect

The wind blows. This is the cause.

What are the effects?

Cause-and-Effect Chart

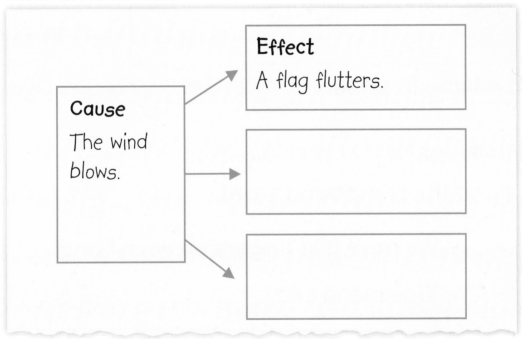

Cause
The wind blows.

Effect
A flag flutters.

Use your cause-and-effect chart. Tell a partner facts you learned in *I Face the Wind*.

A flag flutters because the wind blows.

Compound Words

Touch your nose with your fingertips.

finger + tips = fingertips < compound word

Learn the meanings of both words to understand the **compound word**.

finger • We have five **fingers** on each hand.

+ tips • **Tips** mean ends.

fingertips • **Fingertips** are the ends of fingers.

Try It Together

rain	+	coat	=	raincoat
sun	+	glasses	=	sunglasses
snow	+	man	=	snowman

Talk about the meaning of each compound word.
Use the two shorter words to help you. Then draw a picture to show the compound word.
Label your drawing.

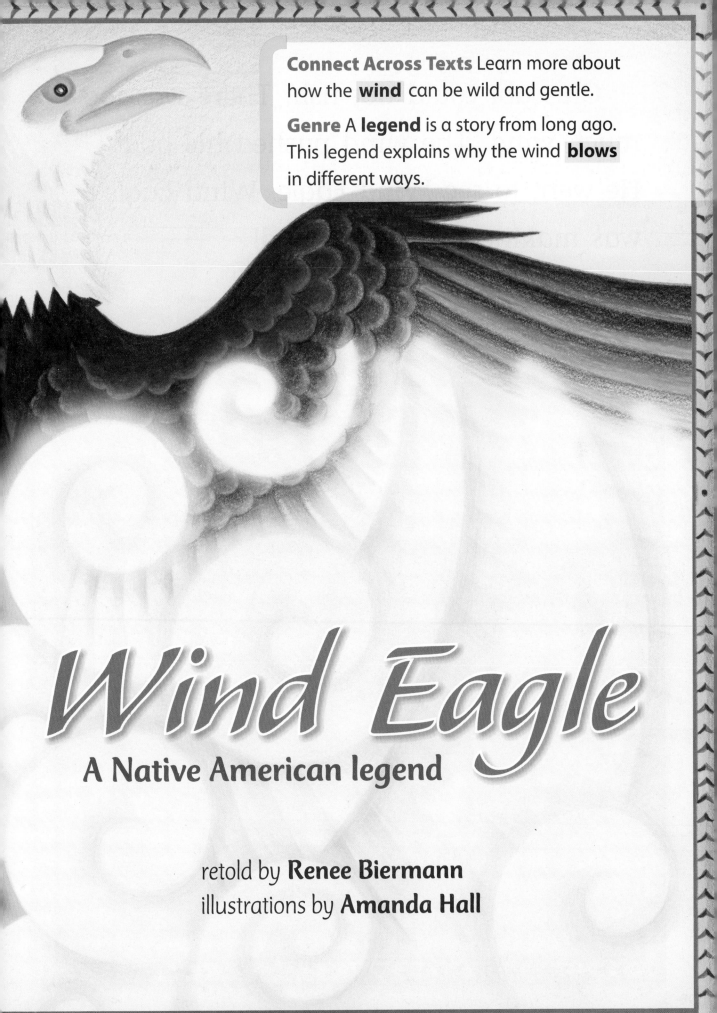

Connect Across Texts Learn more about how the **wind** can be wild and gentle.

Genre A **legend** is a story from long ago. This legend explains why the wind **blows** in different ways.

Wind Eagle
A Native American legend

retold by **Renee Biermann**
illustrations by **Amanda Hall**

Gluscabi could not fish. There was too much wind. The wind pushed his boat. He went to see Wind Eagle. Wind Eagle was making too much wind!

Gluscabi put Wind Eagle in a hole.
Now there was no wind. Gluscabi
was happy. He could easily fish.

Weeks went by. Bad things started to happen because the wind did not blow. Everyone was hot. The fish began to die. The people in the village were not happy.

Gluscabi went to see Wind Eagle. Wind Eagle promised to make gentle winds. So Gluscabi took Wind Eagle out of the hole.

But on some days Wind Eagle forgets his promise. That's why some days **feel** very windy. ❖

Character's Action

In *Wind Eagle,* what are the reasons for Gluscabi's actions?

Gluscabi's Actions	Reasons
Gluscabi went to see Wind Eagle.	There was too much wind. Gluscabi couldn't fish.
Gluscabi put Wind Eagle in a hole.	
Gluscabi went to see Wind Eagle again.	
Gluscabi took Wind Eagle out of the hole.	

Talk Together

Think about what you read and learned. What's wild about **weather**?

Sentence Types

There are four **types of sentences**.

Grammar Rules Sentence Types	
1. A **statement** tells something. It ends with a **period**.	• Gluscabi could not fish. **period**
2. A **question** asks something. It ends with an **question mark**.	• Can you feel the wind? **question mark**
3. An **exclamation** shows strong feeling. It ends with an **exclamation point**.	• There is too much wind! **exclamation point**
4. A **command** tells someone to do something. It starts with a verb. It ends with a **period** or an **exclamation point**.	• Stop, Wind Eagle! **exclamation point**

Read a Sentence

What types of sentences are these? How do you know?

It was so hot!

The fish began to die.

Write a Sentence

Write a sentence about today's weather.
Read it aloud.

103

High Frequency Words

see

that

think

Express Ideas

Listen and sing.

Watching the Weather

Song

I **see** big, dark clouds today.

I **think that** we will get rain.

I see a bright sun outside.

I think we'll be hot tonight!

I see snow fall from the sky.

I think we'll have a snowball fight!

Tune: "Twinkle Twinkle, Little Star"

104

Key Words

What is the weather?

snowy

rainy

Weather

sunny

cloudy

The weather is different
every **month** of the **year**.

calendar

JANUARY	MAY	SEPTEMBER
FEBRUARY	JUNE	OCTOBER
MARCH	JULY	NOVEMBER
APRIL	AUGUST	DECEMBER

Talk Together

What is the weather like today? Is it wild?

Classify Details

Classification Chart

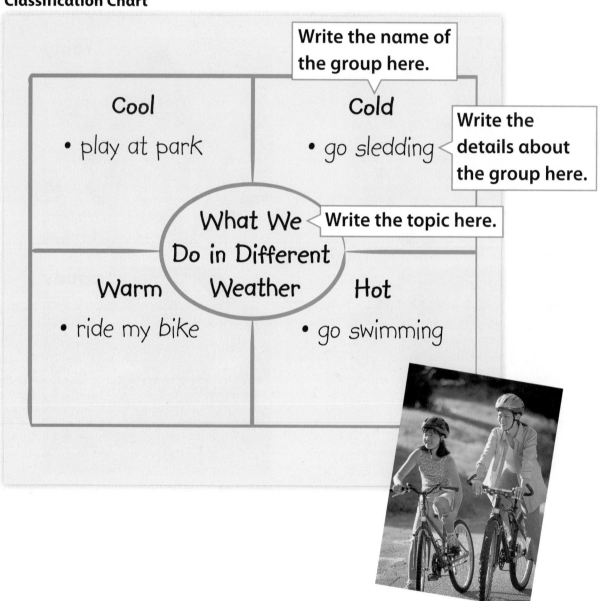

Cool
- play at park

Cold
- go sledding

Write the name of the group here.

Write the details about the group here.

What We Do in Different Weather

Write the topic here.

Warm
- ride my bike

Hot
- go swimming

Talk Together

Tell your partner what you do in different kinds of weather. Add to the classification chart. How is your weather wild?

More Key Words

cold

It's **cold** today.

cool

The fan keeps me **cool**.

hot

The stove is **hot**.

temperature

The **temperature** is 8° Fahrenheit.

warm

The blanket keeps us **warm**.

Talk Together

Ask a question using a **Key Word**.

What do you wear when it is cold outside?

Add words to My Vocabulary Notebook.
NGReach.com

Read Realistic Fiction

Realistic fiction is a story that is made up, but could happen in real life.

Sensory Details

Sensory details tell what characters see, hear, smell, taste, and touch.

sensory detail

February is cold and still.

Reading Strategy

Make inferences as you read. How do you think Kiko feels about the different weather?

A Year for Kiko

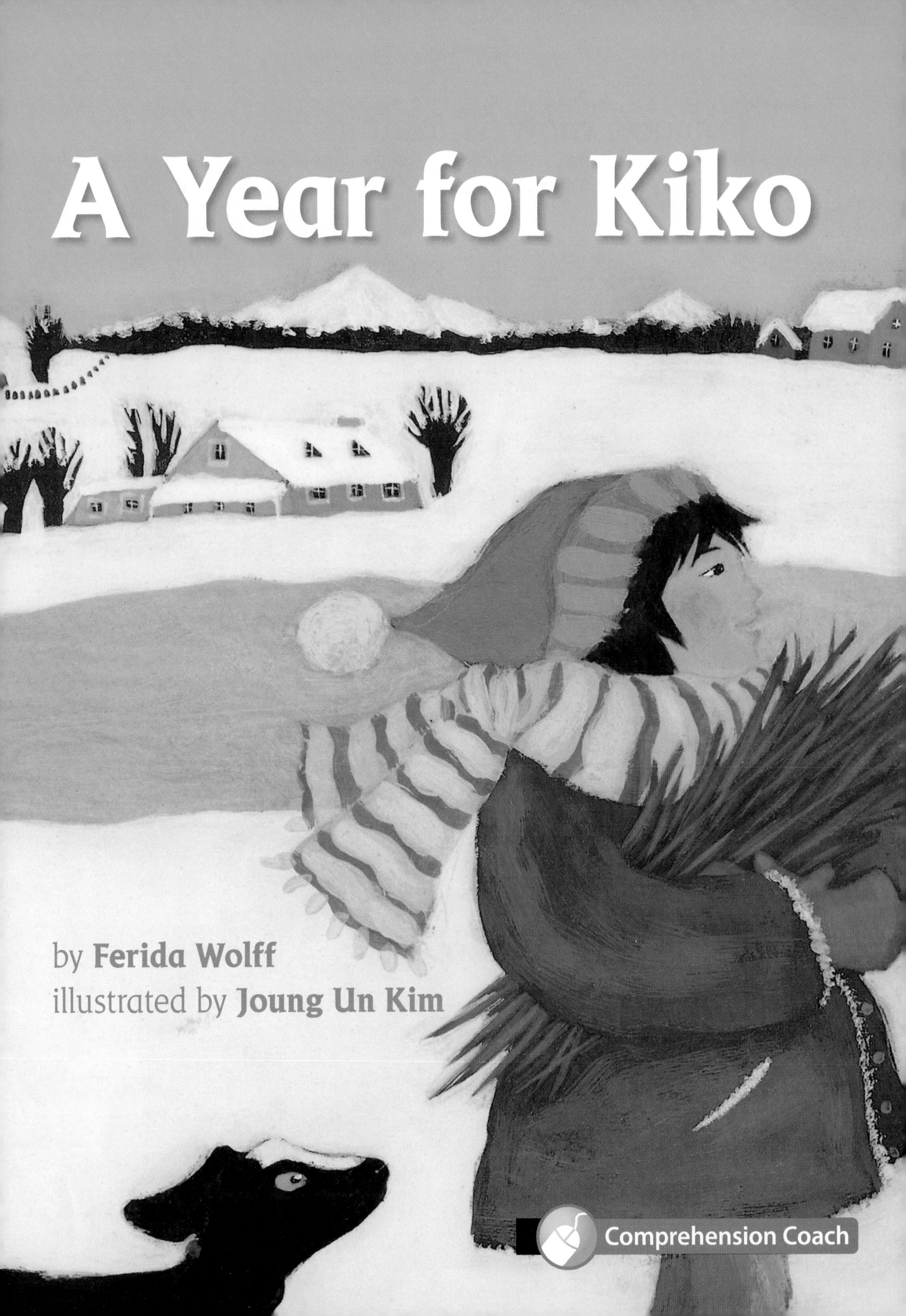

by **Ferida Wolff**

illustrated by **Joung Un Kim**

Comprehension Coach

January **snow** is falling.
Kiko slips in the snow.

February is **cold** and still. Kiko's window is frosted white. Kiko draws a smile with her finger. The smile melts the ice.

Kiko's hat flies off! March
wind whips Kiko's hair.
"I am the wind," says Kiko.

112

April **rain** falls everywhere. It waters the earth and Kiko, too. Now she must play inside.

Kiko plants a seed. Maybe it will grow big. May is a **month** for growing.

Kiko picks June strawberries. One fat berry for the basket. Many fat berries for Kiko. Inside they become Kikoberries.

July fireflies glow in the night. They blink their lights at Kiko. Kiko chases them and laughs. Her eyes are shining, too.

August mornings are **hot**. Kiko wears her bathing suit. She sits in her pool. Now August feels **cool**.

Crickets chirp at Kiko. Together they sing a September song.

Red and gold leaves are falling. Kiko holds a red leaf in one hand. She holds a gold leaf in the other. Kiko feels like an October tree.

Kiko looks for the moon. The orange moon is hiding. When Kiko hides, the moon finds her. Kiko and the November moon are playing.

In December Kiko breathes out
clouds. She puts on her winter coat.
She wears her mittens and hat.
Kiko is ready for snow. ❖

Meet the Author

Ferida Wolff

Ferida Wolff wrote a lot when she was a young girl. She wrote about people and pets. She wrote letters and stories.

Ms. Wolff still writes many stories. There is always something new to learn and write about.

▲ Ferida Wolff

Writer's Craft

Find words that Ferida Wolff used to tell what Kiko does. Can you think of other action words?

Talk About It

1. What does Kiko do in the **month** of May?

Kiko _____ in the month of May.

2. Why does Kiko wear a hat and gloves when she plays in the **snow**?

She wears them because _____ .

3. Does Kiko like July? How do you know?

Kiko _____ July. She _____ .

Learn test-taking strategies.
⊘ NGReach.com

Write About It

Find one sensory detail in *A Year for Kiko*.
Fill in these sentences.

The sensory detail word is _____ .
This tells me Kiko _____ .

Classify Details

What does Kiko do in different weather?

Classification Chart

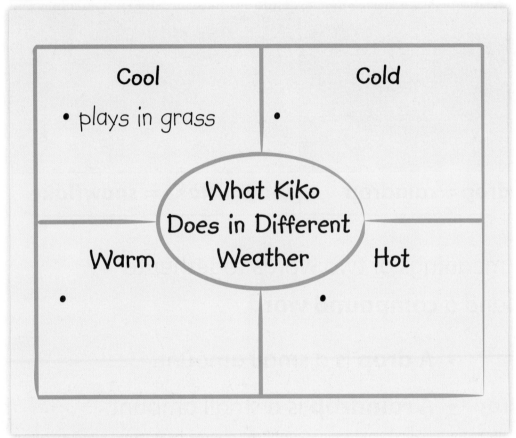

Cool
- plays in grass

Cold
-

What Kiko Does in Different Weather

Warm
-

Hot
-

Use your chart and the illustrations in the story to retell what Kiko does in different weather.

Compound Words

raindrop	snowflake
rain + drop = raindrop	snow + flake = snowflake

Put the meanings of two words together to understand a **compound word**.

drop
- A **drop** is a small amount.

rain + drop
- A **raindrop** is a small amount of rain.

Try It Together

Put these words together to make compound words. Use what you know about each word to tell what it means.

fire	+	flies	=	fireflies
Kiko	+	berries	=	Kikoberries
moon	+	light	=	moonlight

NATIONAL
GEOGRAPHIC
EXCLUSIVE

Connect Across Texts Learn more about how weather can be wild.

Genre In an **interview**, one person asks questions while another person answers them.

Chasing Storms
with Tim Samaras

by **Jennifer Tetzloff**

Most people run from tornadoes. Not Tim Samaras. He is a storm chaser.

What is a storm chaser?

A storm chaser follows thunderstorms that create tornadoes to learn more about them.

What is a tornado?

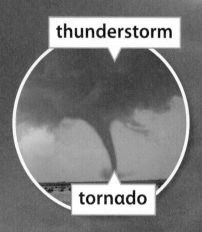

thunderstorm

tornado

A tornado starts as a powerful thunderstorm. The storm creates spinning, funnel-shaped clouds. If the clouds touch the ground, then it is a tornado.

Where and when do tornadoes happen?

Tornadoes can happen anywhere. Most tornadoes happen between March and August.

Why do you study tornadoes?

Tornadoes are dangerous. Learning about tornadoes helps keep people safe. ❖

Compare Genres

How are the words in *A Year for Kiko* and "Chasing Storms with Tim Samaras" different?

Realistic Fiction

July fireflies glow in the night. They blink their lights at Kiko. Kiko chases them and laughs. Her eyes are shining, too.

116

Interview

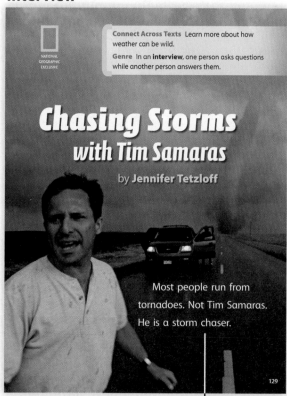

Connect Across Texts Learn more about how weather can be wild.

Genre In an **interview**, one person asks questions while another person answers them.

Chasing Storms
with Tim Samaras
by **Jennifer Tetzloff**

Most people run from tornadoes. Not Tim Samaras. He is a storm chaser.

129

has sensory details and characters

has facts about real people

Talk Together

Think about what you read. What's wild about weather?

Ask Questions

Ask a **question** to get **information**.

Grammar Rules Ask Questions

Questions	Information
Who is that?	That is Tim.
What is that?	It is a tornado.
Where is the tornado?	It is far away.
Why is it so windy?	It is windy because of the tornado.
When did it start raining?	It started at 4:00.
How is the weather?	It is rainy.

Read a Sentence

What information do these questions ask about?
How do you know?

1. Who is a storm chaser?
2. When can I meet Tim?

Write a Sentence

Write a question for Tim. Ask him for information about his job.

133

Write Like a Reporter

Write a Nonfiction Paragraph

What do you know about weather? Explain what happens on a windy, rainy, sunny, or snowy day. Write a paragraph for your classmates.

A Rainy Day

> A paragraph has an indent.

Kids wear raincoats. They jump in puddles. You hear thunder. Boom! This all happens because the weather is rainy. Rain falls from the sky.

A nonfiction paragraph tells something real that happens.

It also tells why things happen.

❶ Plan and Write

Talk about kinds of weather with a partner. Pick one kind of weather. Explain to your partner what happens because of this weather.

Write a sentence that tells the kind of weather. Then write sentences to explain what happens because of this weather.

❷ Check Your Work

Revise and edit your writing. Use this checklist.

❸ Finish and Share

Finish your paragraph. Write each sentence neatly. Leave space between each word.

Read your paragraph clearly. Listen politely when other reporters read.

Checklist

- ☑ Did you use any compound words? Can you add one?

- ☑ Check your sentences. Did you use the right end marks?

- ☑ Read each word of your paragraph. Check the spelling. Look for missing letters. Correct spelling errors.

Sometimes we hear thunder on a rainy day.

Share Your Ideas

Think about the different kinds of weather. What's wild about weather? Choose one of these ways to share your ideas about the **Big Question**.

Write It!

Draw and Write
Draw a picture of a storm. Write two sentences about the storm. Tell how it looks and sounds.

The sky is dark. The thunder is loud.

Talk About It!

Weather Report

Pretend that you are a weather person on TV. Give your weather report to the group. Describe the weather today. Tell what the weather will be like tomorrow.

> Today it is sunny and warm.

Do It!

Make Air Move

With a partner make a fan, kite, or other type of air mover. Explain to your partner how your invention works.

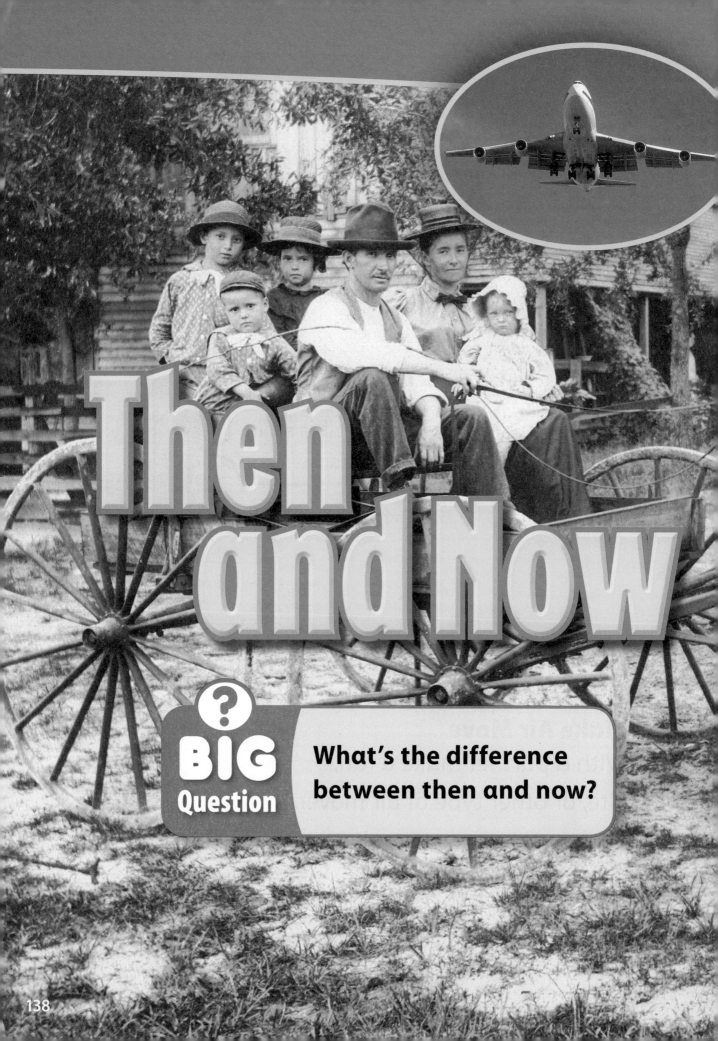

Then and Now

BIG Question

What's the difference between then and now?

Unit at a Glance
▶ **Language**: Express Opinions, Express Feelings, Social Studies Words
▶ **Literacy**: Visualize
▶ **Content**: Then and Now

Unit
7

Share What You Know

Do It!

❶ **Act Out** something you do with a machine. Let the class guess.

❷ **Discuss** what people did before they had that machine.

Build Background: Watch a video about an invention.
NGReach.com

Express Opinions

Listen and sing. *Song* (((MP3)))

I think it would be great
To hear your voice.
I think it would be great
To hear your voice.

You could write a letter.
But I think
The phone is better.

I do not think a letter
Is a good choice.

Tune: "If You're Happy and You Know It"

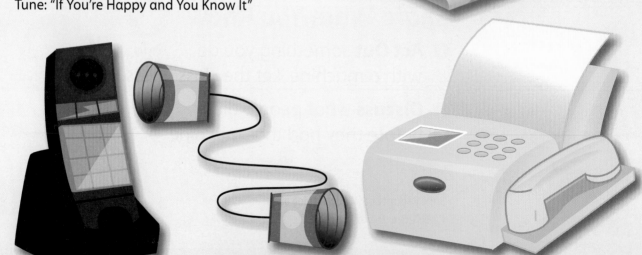

Key Words

How do people talk and share **news**?

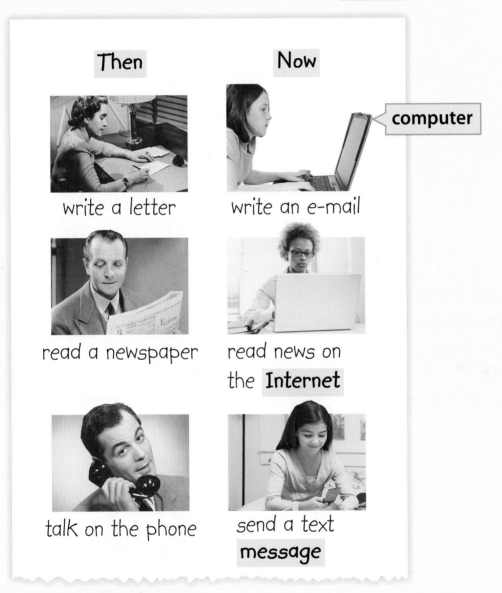

Then

Now

computer

write a letter

write an e-mail

read a newspaper

read news on the **Internet**

talk on the phone

send a text **message**

Talk Together

Look at the ways we communicate. What's the difference between then and now? What do you think is the best way to communicate?

Identify Main Idea and Details

Main Idea and Details Diagram

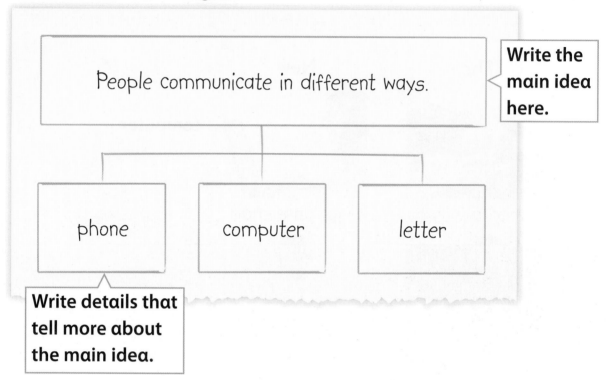

People communicate in different ways.

> Write the main idea here.

phone   computer   letter

> Write details that tell more about the main idea.

Look for the main idea and details as you listen and read.

Talk Together

Use gestures to show how you communicate. Your partner guesses what you are doing. Take turns. Then add ways you communicate to the chart.

More Key Words

past — present — future

past

present

future

In the **past** I was in kindergarten.

Today is the **present**. I am in first grade.

In the **future** I will be in second grade.

communicate

People **communicate** by talking and writing.

history

Study **history** to learn what happened long ago.

Talk Together

Make **Key Word** cards. Pick one, and use the word in a sentence.

I learn about the present by watching today's TV news.

Add words to My Vocabulary Notebook.

NGReach.com

143

Read a History Article

A **history article** is nonfiction. It describes what life was like in the past.

Time Line

A time line shows when things happened.

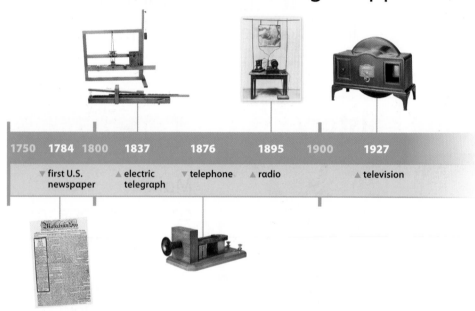

1750	1784	1800	1837	1876	1895	1900	1927
	▼ first U.S. newspaper		▲ electric telegraph	▼ telephone	▲ radio		▲ television

▲ This time line shows years.

Reading Strategy

As you read, use the words and pictures to **visualize** what things were like in the past.

Communication
Then and Now

by **Robin Nelson**

Comprehension Coach

Communication is sharing ideas and news.
Most people communicate by talking and writing.
People can use their bodies to communicate, too.

Communication has changed. People now communicate better and faster.

Long ago, people made pictures to tell stories. The pictures could be drawings or symbols.

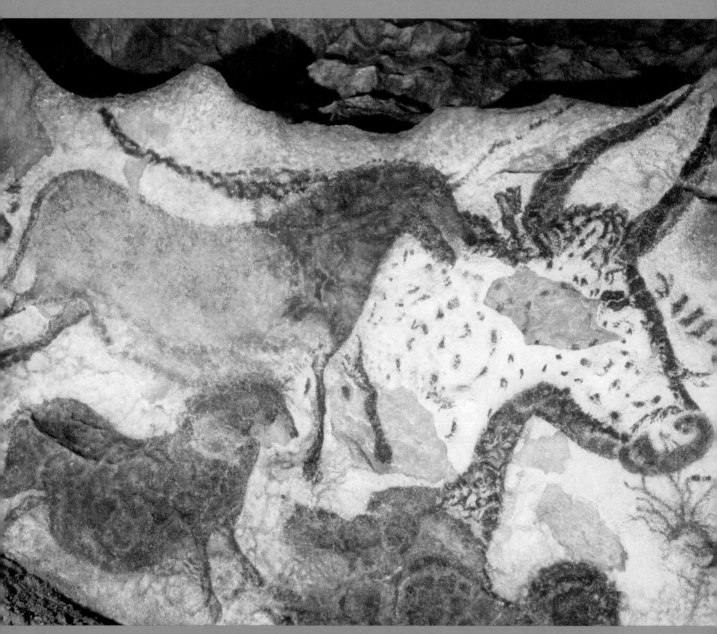

This painting was discovered in a cave in France.

There are over 170,000 words in the English language.

Now, people use words more often
to tell stories.

Long ago, people copied each book.
If they wanted 10 copies of a book, they
had to write out each copy one at a time.

▲ This book was written with a feather
pen and bottles of ink in 1453.

feather pen

ink

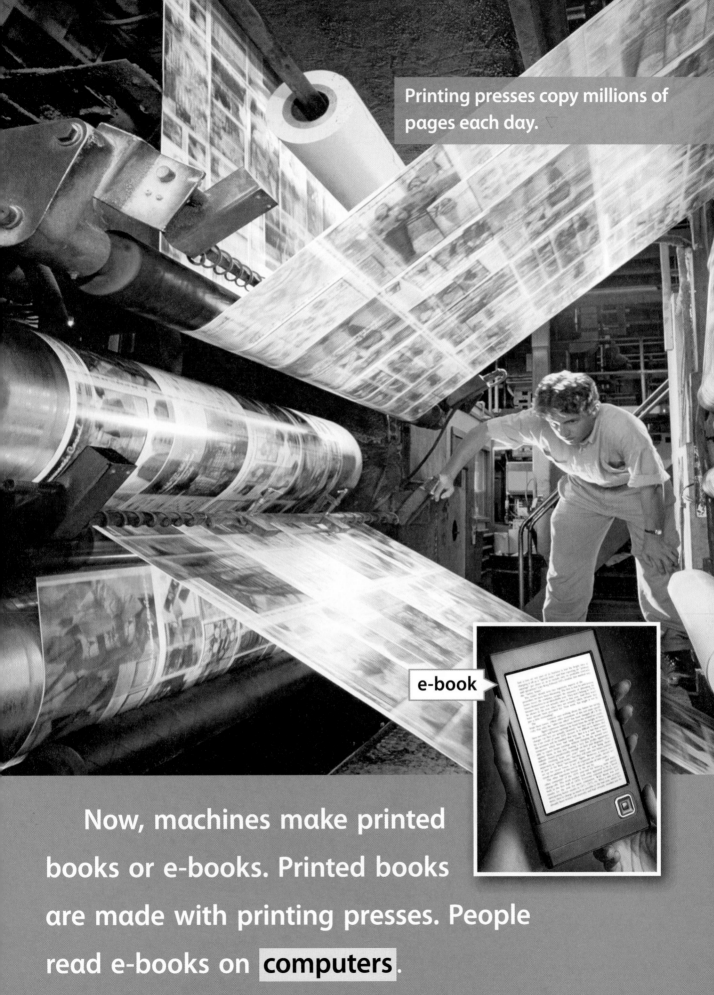

Printing presses copy millions of pages each day.

e-book

Now, machines make printed books or e-books. Printed books are made with printing presses. People read e-books on **computers**.

151

Long ago, people tapped **messages** on telegraph machines. Telegraph machines sent messages using electricity. It took about a minute to send each word.

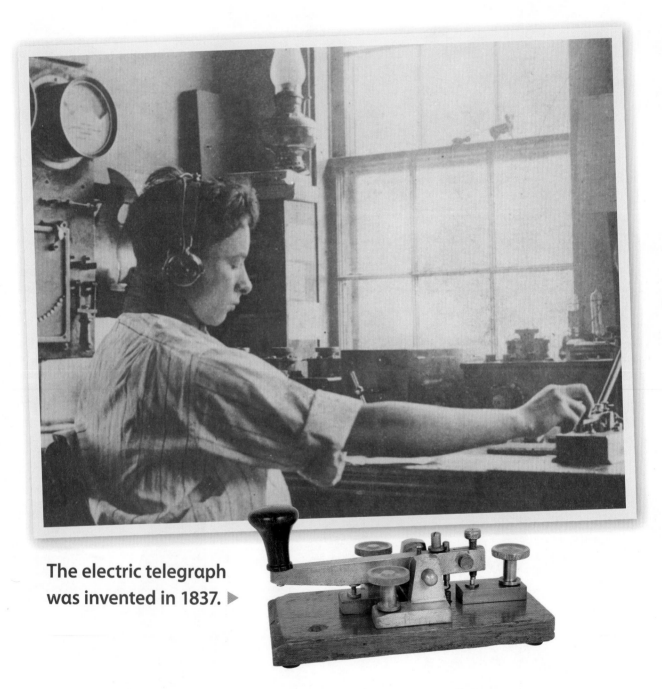

The electric telegraph was invented in 1837. ▶

mobile phone

The telephone was invented in 1876 by Alexander Graham Bell.

cord

Now, people call each other on telephones. Most people have mobile phones. Long ago, telephones always needed cords.

Long ago, people wrote letters. It could take months to mail a letter. Mail went on ships and by horses. Today, mail delivery is done by trucks and planes so letters are delivered much quicker.

▲ People wrote letters using pens and paper.

ink

ink pen

Now, people write e-mails on computers. An e-mail message can be delivered in just seconds. Today, many people write e-mail messages instead of hand-written letters.

e-mail message

155

Newspapers were sold on street corners. This newspaper was sold in New York in 1896.

Long ago, hundreds of people read newspapers. The first United States daily newspaper was published in 1784. People had to buy a newspaper to read it.

Many people get newspapers delivered to them at home.

Now, millions of people read newspapers. People can buy printed newspapers.

People can also read newspapers on the **Internet**. People all over the world can read news on the Internet.

Internet news

laptop computer

Long ago, people could only listen to news on radios. Radios only make sounds. They do not have pictures.

△ The radio was invented in 1895.

Now, people can watch news on televisions.

Communication will continue to change. What do you think will happen next? ❖

The TV was invented in 1927. ▷

Communication Timeline

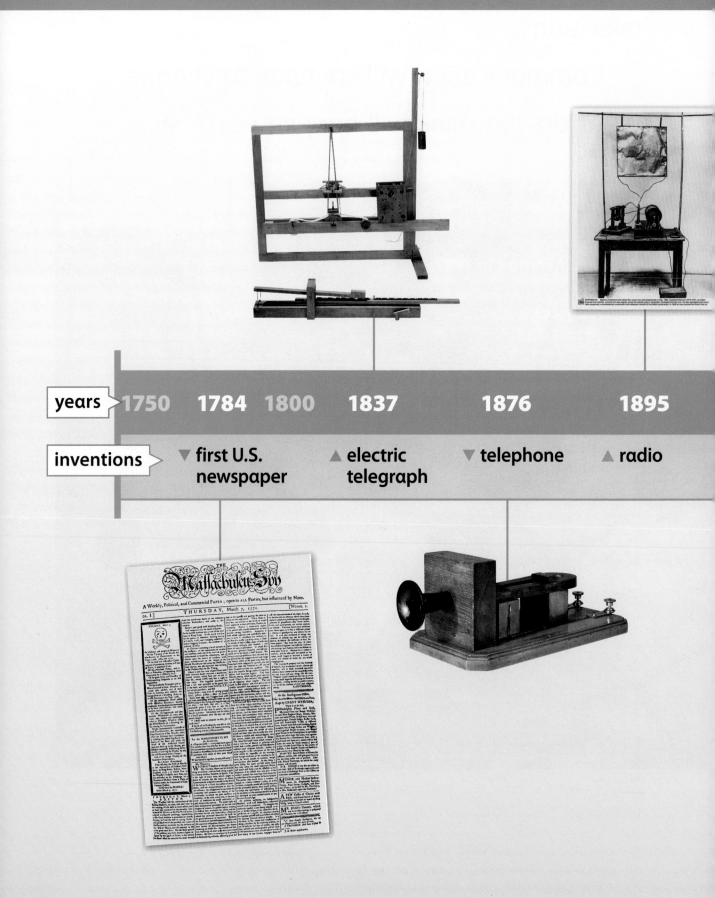

years	1750	1784	1800	1837	1876	1895

inventions	▼ first U.S. newspaper	▲ electric telegraph	▼ telephone	▲ radio

| 1900 | 1927 | 1943 | 1972 | 1985 | 2000 |

▲ television ▼ computer ▲ e-mail ▼ first cell
phones used

Talk About It

1. How do people **communicate**?

People communicate by ____ and ____ .

2. How is communication different **now** than it was in the **past**? Look back in the text and name two details.

Now, people ____ . Then, people ____ .

3. Why is the **computer** an important invention?

People can ____ and ____ on a computer.

Learn test-taking strategies.
NGReach.com

Write About It

What is your favorite way to communicate? Why?

I like to ____ because ____ .

Identify Main Idea and Details

Add details to show how communication has changed.

Main Idea and Details Diagram

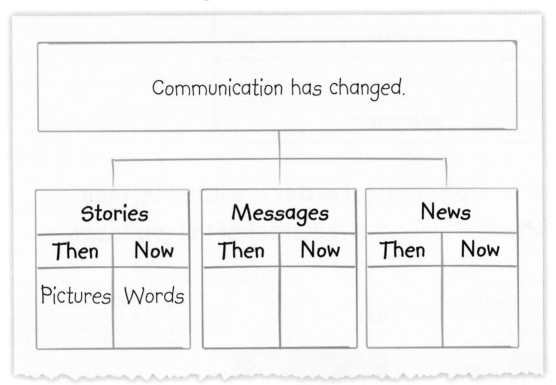

Communication has changed.					
Stories		**Messages**		**News**	
Then	Now	Then	Now	Then	Now
Pictures	Words				

Use your chart to tell how communication has changed.

"Long ago, people drew stories with pictures."

"Now, people write stories with words."

163

Alphabetize and Use a Dictionary

Words in Alphabetical Order
computer
e-mail
radio
telegraph

Words in **alphabetical order** are listed by their first letters. They go in the order of the alphabet.

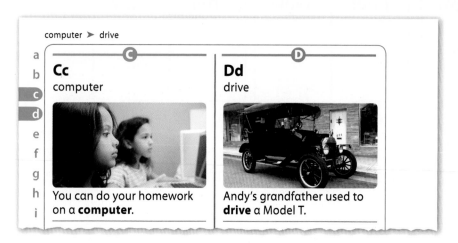

Try It Together

With a partner, put these words in alphabetical order. Use a dictionary to find each word's meaning.

telephone
newspaper
book
machine

NATIONAL
GEOGRAPHIC
EXCLUSIVE

Connect Across Texts You read about **communication** **now** and in the **past**. Now read about inventions for the **future**.

Genre A **blog** is an **Internet** journal. This **blog entry** is nonfiction. It gives information about space inventions.

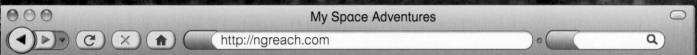

My Space Adventures

http://ngreach.com

My Space Adventures

MAIN SCREEN | PICTURES | LINKS | SIGN IN

Date: August 21

Building for Space

My name is Constance Adams. I make things to use in space.

Search

LINKS

▸ Space News

▸ Astronaut News

▲ Astronauts train for space travel in this model.

MAIN SCREEN | PICTURES | LINKS | SIGN IN

Space is not like earth. The air is different. People have to wear special clothing. They bring air to breathe. People float around in space. It is fun to watch!

Search

LINKS

▸ Space News

▸ Astronaut News

▶ **Read More** About Astronauts

I make new inventions to use in space.
I am helping to build a spaceship that
astronauts will fly to the moon.

moon

Next »

MAIN SCREEN | PICTURES | LINKS | SIGN IN

The first spaceship that flew to the moon did not have much power. One **computer** in your classroom has more power than that spaceship did! Now, we can make more powerful spaceships.

Search

LINKS

▸ Space News

▸ Astronaut News

Then: The Apollo 11 spaceship in 1969.

It is fun to imagine what we will be able to make in the future!

Now: This is a computer drawing of a future spaceship being worked on. It is called Ares.

Posted by Constance Adams   August 24 9:00 a.m. ❖

4 COMMENTS

Older Posts »

Compare Genres

Think about *Communication Then and Now* and "My Space Adventures." How are they alike and different?

Venn Diagram

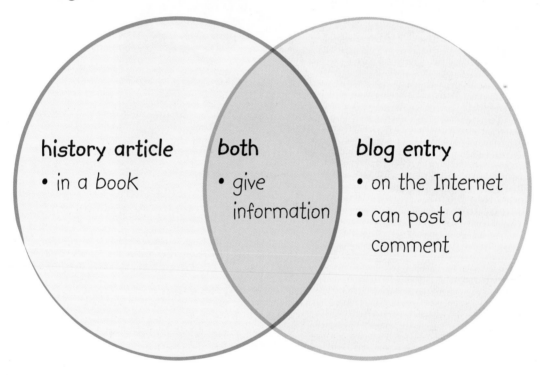

history article
• in a book

both
• give information

blog entry
• on the Internet
• can post a comment

Look through the texts. Add to the diagram.

Talk Together

Think about what you read and learned. What's the difference between **then** and **now**?

Past Tense Verbs

Verbs can tell about actions that happened in the past.

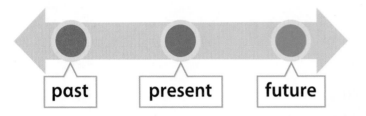

| past | present | future |

Grammar Rules Past Tense Verbs

To make a verb about the past:	Today people **want** to build new spaceships. In the past, they **wanted** to build the first spaceship.
• Add -**ed** to the end of a **regular verb**, like **want**.	
• Use a special form for an **irregular verb**, like **fly**.	Today people **fly** to space. In the past, they **flew** to space for the first time.

Read a Sentence

Read page 150. Find two verbs in the past tense. Explain their form.

Write a Sentence

Write a sentence about a time you wanted to go somewhere new. Read it to a partner.

**High Frequency
Words**

am

could

feel

Express Feelings

Listen and Sing.   *Song* ((MP3))

New Phone

Oh, my darling. I am Marta.
My new phone is very small.
I wish I could have my old phone.
It was always on the wall.

My new phone is very modern.
I feel really glad for this.
I wish I could use my new phone,
But I don't know where it is.

Tune: "My Darling Clementine"

Key Words

Old

New

The old **record** player is fun to use.

But the new way to play **music** sounds **better**. It is **easier** to carry with you.

Talk Together

How would you feel about listening to music on a record player? Are new ways always better?

Describe Characters' Feelings

Character Description Chart

Character	What the Character Says or Does	What this Shows About How the Character Feels
Marta	• I wish I could have my old phone. • I feel very glad for this.	• unhappy • happy

| Write the name of the character here. | Write what the character says or does here. | Write how the character feels here. |

I feel sad that I don't have those shoes anymore.

Talk Together

What do you wish you could have from the past? Describe your feelings about it to a partner.

More Key Words

build

You can **build** things with blocks.

invent

People **invent** things like the telephone.

machine

This **machine** washes dishes.

modern

This cell phone is more **modern** than the old phone.

tool

Dictionary

People use a dictionary as a **tool** to understand words.

Talk Together

Draw a picture of a **Key Word** for a partner to label.

tool

Add words to My Vocabulary Notebook.
NGReach.com

Read a Story

Realistic fiction has events that are not real but could happen in real life.

Characters' Feelings

Look for words that tell you how characters feel. Then think about why the characters have these feelings.

feeling word

"I love music just like you do."

Reading Strategy

As you read, use the words and pictures to **visualize** how the characters feel and why.

A New Old Tune

by **Pat Cummings**

illustrated by
Frank Morrison

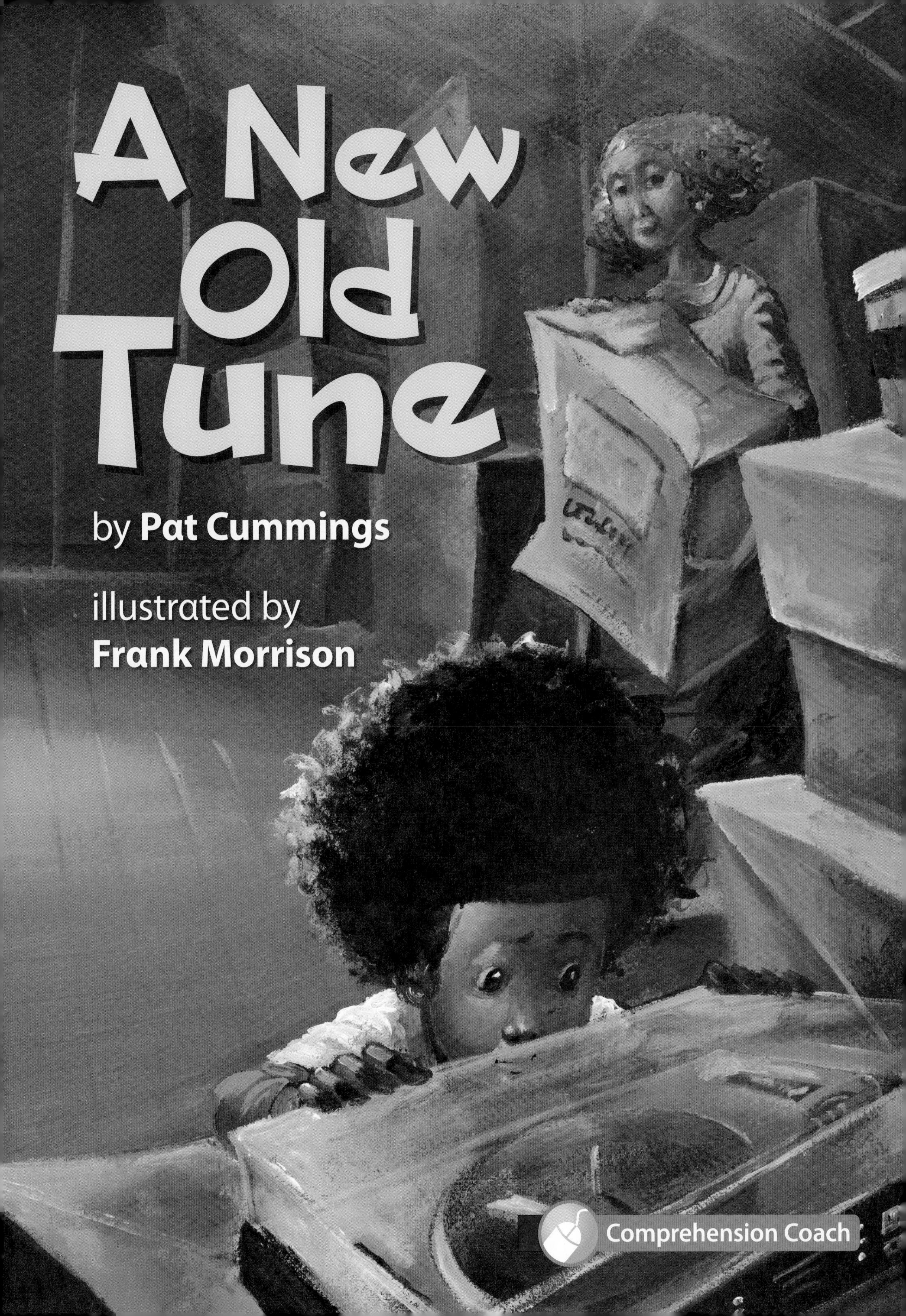

Comprehension Coach

"What is this, Aunt Nell?" asked Max. He was helping his aunt choose things to sell at her yard sale.

"This disk must go into a giant computer!" Max said. Aunt Nell shook her head.

"That is a **record**," Aunt Nell said.
"I love **music** just like you do."

Aunt Nell pulled out a stack of
black disks.

"Wow," said Max. "How do
they work?"

Aunt Nell opened a dusty, wooden box. She plugged it into the wall. "This is my old record player."

Music filled the attic.
"But you can't carry it with you!" Max said.

"No one carried music players back then," Aunt Nell said. "I played music on this record player at home. My friends would listen, too. Then we would dance together."

"Things change," Aunt Nell said.
"Television used to be just black and white."

"You had TV way back then?"
Max asked.

"Hey, I'm not that old!" Aunt Nell said.

Max and Aunt Nell got back
to work. There was an old camera
she wanted to sell. There were
photo albums she wanted to keep.

Max saw a picture of a young Aunt Nell talking on a phone. It had a long, curly cord.

"Did you like those old phones **better**?" Max asked.

"No," Aunt Nell smiled. "Some **new** things are much **easier** to use."

"But some old things are pretty neat," Max said. He looked at the record player. "Will you dance with me?" Max asked.

"Yes," said Aunt Nell. She turned up the music.

"Has anything stayed the same?" asked Max.

"Yes," said Aunt Nell. "People still love to talk on the telephone. And watch television. And listen to music."

"And dance!" added Max.

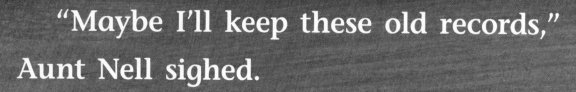

"Maybe I'll keep these old records," Aunt Nell sighed.

"Or you could burn them onto a music player," Max said.

"BURN them?" Aunt Nell gasped.

Max groaned. It was his turn to explain.

Pat Cummings

AWARD
WINNER

Pat Cummings moved often when she was young. Her father was in the army. She used to draw pictures all the time. She joined art clubs to meet new friends.

Ms. Cummings writes about things she knows. She is always thinking about her next story!

Pat Cummings ▶

Writer's Craft

Pat Cummings helps readers learn about her characters' feelings by using verbs. Can you find examples of this in the story?

Talk About It

1. What was Max helping Aunt Nell do?

Max was helping Aunt Nell _____ .

2. How are Max and Aunt Nell the same?
What do they both like?

Max and Aunt Nell both like _____ .

3. Think about your own photos. Why does
Aunt Nell want to keep her photo albums?

Aunt Nell wants to keep them because _____ .

Learn test-taking strategies.
NGReach.com

Write About It

What does your family own that is **old**?
What do you think about it?

We have an old _____ . I think it is _____ .

Describe Characters' Feelings

What do Max and Nell say or do? What does this show about how they feel?

Character Description Chart

Character	What the Character Says or Does	What This Shows About How the Character Feels
Max	• Wow •	• He feels surprised. •
Nell	• •	• •

Use your chart to talk about Max and Nell. Why do they feel like they do?

Alphabetize and Use a Dictionary

Words in Alphabetical Order

camera

cell phone

cord

These words are in **alphabetical order**. Each word begins with the same letter. The second letter of each word is used to put them in order.

camera ➤ cell phone

a
b
c
d
e
f
g
h
i

Cc
camera

Amy likes taking pictures with her dad's **camera**.

cell phone

Many people use **cell phones** now.

Try It Together

With a partner, write these words on cards. Put the words in alphabetical order. Use a dictionary to find the word's meaning. Then read your list aloud.

music
modern
machine

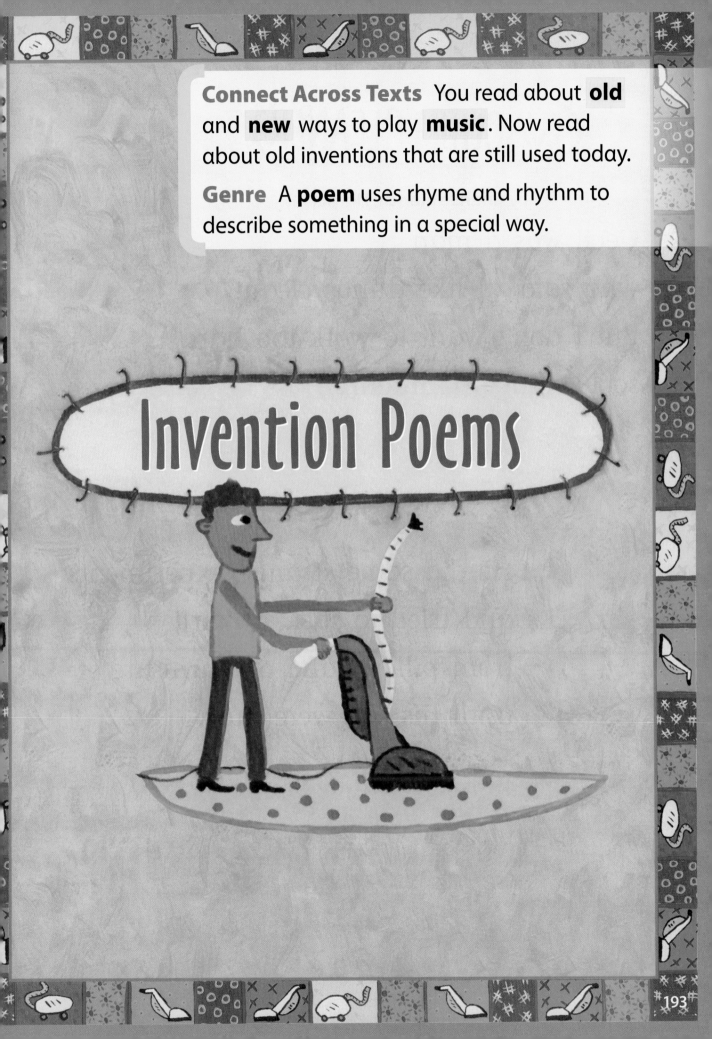

Connect Across Texts You read about **old** and **new** ways to play **music**. Now read about old inventions that are still used today.

Genre A **poem** uses rhyme and rhythm to describe something in a special way.

Invention Poems

VACUUM CLEANER

by **Charise Mericle Harper**

Cecil was a man
who said, "I like things clean!
But I don't want to work too hard,
so I'll make a **machine**."

He did some strange experiments
and tried to suck up dirt,
from pillows and on furniture
until his lips were hurt.

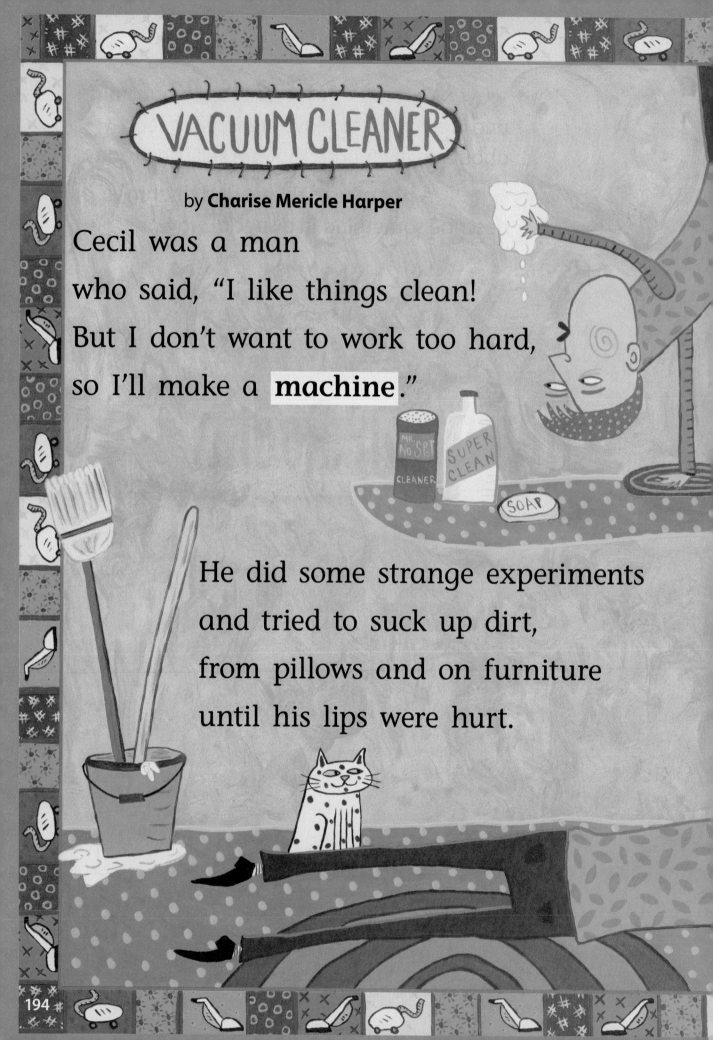

MINI BROOM DUSTPAN FEATHER DUSTER

And then he tried some blowing,
but said, "No, that seems wrong!
I think I need a wind machine
that sucks up dirt real strong."

DIRTY CLEAN

1901 was the year
that he built his first machine.
It took two men to operate
but really got things clean.

THEN

NOW

Past and Present

by **Hector Sanchez**

When I think about
The present and the past,
I think about machines
That move slow and fast.

Clunky cars used to creep
So super slow,
Now they zip and zoom
And go, go, go!

Compare Genres

A New Old Tune is realistic fiction. "Vacuum Cleaner" and "Past and Present" are poems. Find connections between these texts.

Realistic Fiction

"No one carried music players back then," Aunt Nell said. "I played music on this record player at home. My friends would listen, too. Then we would dance together."

182

Poem

VACUUM CLEANER

by **Charise Mericle Harper**

Cecil was a man
who said, "I like things clean!
But I don't want to work too hard,
so I'll make a **machine**."

He did some strange experiments
and tried to suck up dirt,
from pillows and on furniture
until his lips were hurt.

194

> They both talk about things from the past.

Talk Together

Talk about what life was like before **machines**. What is the difference between then and now?

Future Tense Verbs

Some **verbs** tell about actions that will happen in the future.

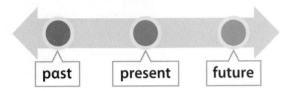

past | present | future

Grammar Rules Future Tense Verbs

To make verbs about the future:	
• Add **will** before the verb.	• He **will** invent.
Add these verbs after the subject and before the main verb: • I **am going to** • He/She/It **is going to** • They **are going to**	• He **is going to** make a machine.

Read a Sentence

Does this sentence tell about the future? Explain.

Cecil will make a new machine.

Write a Sentence

Write a sentence about what machines will do in the future. Read it to a partner.

Write as a Friend

Write a Friendly Letter

What do you know about things from the past? Describe something old you have seen. Write a letter to a friend.

October 1

Dear Manny,

    Last week, my dad showed me an old phone. The old phone did not have buttons. It had a dial with numbers. It had holes for your fingers.

    The next day, I took the phone to school. We all dialed our phone numbers! I think old things are fun to use.

Your friend,
Altagracia

Write your friend's name in the **greeting**.

In the **body** of the letter, tell your news. This could include a **main idea** and details.

Write a **closing** and sign your name.

❶ Plan and Write

Talk about things from the past with a partner. Draw a picture of one old thing. Write a list of details. Discuss your main idea. Tell your partner what you think about old things.

Write the main idea. Then write sentences with details. Remember to express your opinion.

❷ Check Your Work

Revise and edit your writing. Use this checklist.

❸ Finish and Share

Finish your letter. Make sure the greeting and other features of a letter are correct.

Read your letter to a friend. Share your opinions.

Checklist

☑ Think about different words you can use. Can you use compound words, synonyms, or antonyms?

☑ Did you use past tense and future tense verbs correctly?

☑ Trade work with a partner. Check for words that sound alike. Does the word meaning make sense in the sentence?

I think old things are too slow.

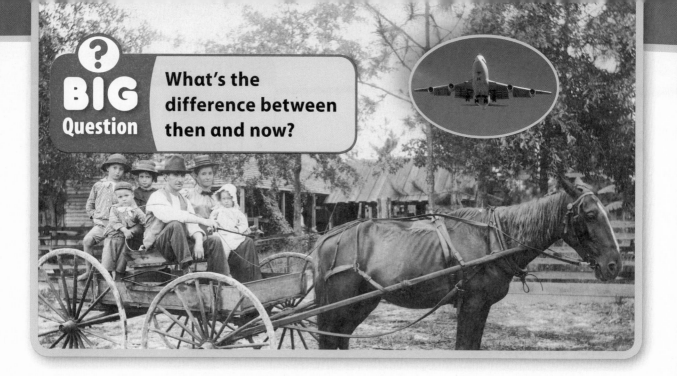

Share Your Ideas

Think about how we do things now and how we did things in the past. What's the difference between then and now? Choose one of these ways to share your ideas about the **Big Question**.

Write It!

Alphabetize a List

Write a list of all the **Key Words** from the unit. Then write the words again in alphabetical order. Alphabetize to the first or second letter. Use 3 of the words to write about things you learned about the past.

Talk About It!

Interview a Time Traveler

Pretend you are a time traveler. You are from the past. What is life like? What do you do? Have the group ask you questions. Then have another student pretend to be from the future. Ask more questions.

> I am from the past. I walk to school. We don't have a bus.

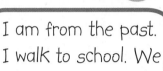

Do It!

Make a Telephone

Have your teacher make a hole in the bottoms of two cans. Put one piece of string through both holes. Tie knots inside the cans to hold the string. Pull the cans apart until the string is tight. One partner listens while the other partner talks.

Get Out the Map!

? BIG Question

Why do we need maps?

Unit
8

Share What You Know

1 **Draw** your classroom

Do It!

2 **Show** where you sit. Show the door.

3 **Use** your drawing to give directions to a partner.

Build Background: Watch a video about maps.
NGReach.com

Follow Directions

Listen and sing. **Song**

High Frequency
Words
left
right
show
turn

At the ZOO

 Oh, dear! Where
Can the monkeys be?

Turn left. Turn right.
And you will see.

 Show me. Where
Can the monkeys be?

This map can
Show you the way.

Tune: "Oh, Dear, What Can the Matter Be?"

You Are Here!

Key Words

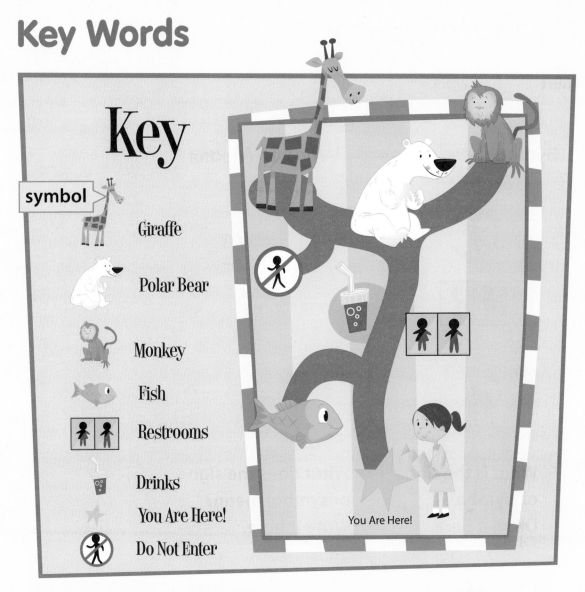

A **map key** is **useful**. It tells the **meaning** of a map's symbols. A symbol or sign can be a shape or a **picture**.

Talk Together

Tell a partner how to go from the entrance to see the fish. Use the map to help. Was the map useful?

207

Use Information

T Chart

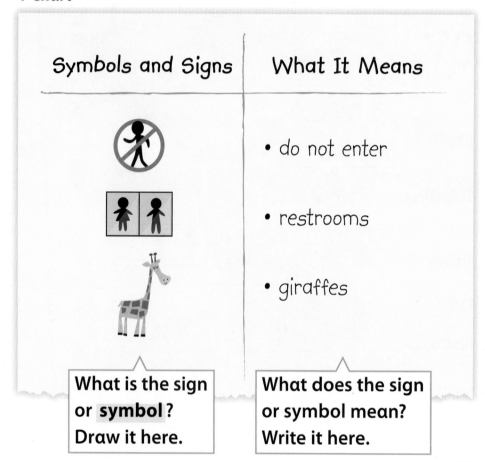

Symbols and Signs	What It Means
	• do not enter
	• restrooms
	• giraffes

What is the sign or symbol? Draw it here.

What does the sign or symbol mean? Write it here.

Talk Together

Talk about the signs and symbols you see in your town. Draw two of them. Add them to the chart above.

More Key Words

• between

The house is **between** the two trees.

corner

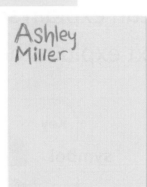

Ashley Miller

I write my name in the **corner** of the paper.

distance

This man runs a long **distance**.

• show

I **show** my drawing.

sign

This **sign** means to add.

Talk Together

Use a **Key Word** to ask a question about maps.

What is the distance from your house to school?

Add words to My Vocabulary Notebook.
NGReach.com

• High Frequency Word

209

Read Informational Text

Informational text can explain something. This informational text explains how maps work.

Maps

Maps use **symbols**. Symbols are pictures or shapes that stand for real things.

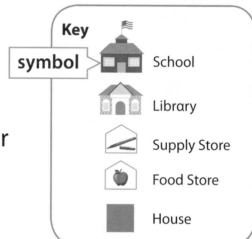

Key

symbol — School

Library

Supply Store

Food Store

House

Reading Strategy

As you read, think of the 7 strategies you learned. Which strategies will help you understand the text?

If Maps Could Talk

by **Erika L. Shores**

illustrated by **Annie Bisset**

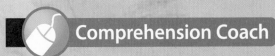

Comprehension Coach

Maps: Finding Your Way

Where is the water slide? If you were a bird, you could fly up high to find it. But since you are not, you will have to use a **map**.

Maps use **symbols** to **show** where things are. The orange rectangle on the **Picture** Map is a symbol for the water slide. How do you know that? Read on.

Picture Map

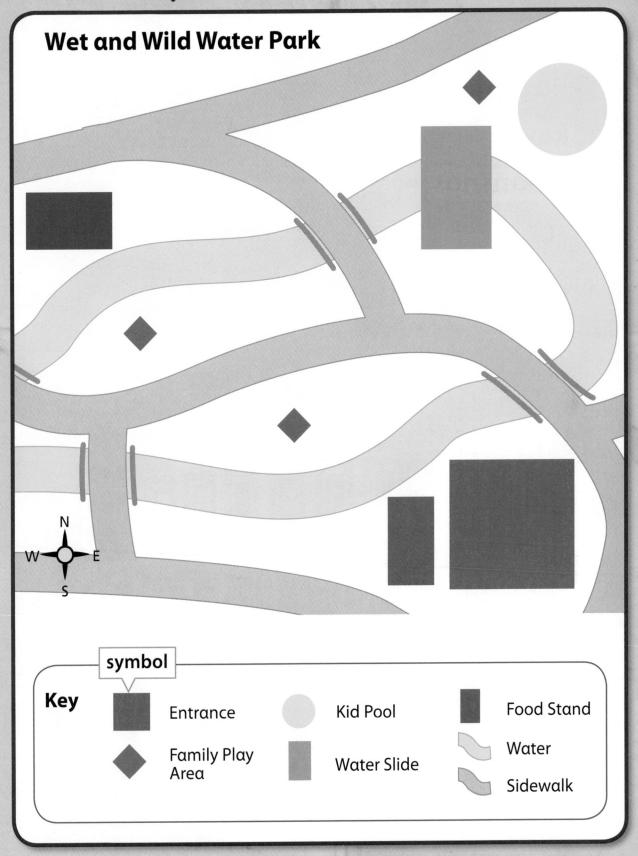

Wet and Wild Water Park

Key

symbol ↓
- ■ Entrance
- ◆ Family Play Area
- ● Kid Pool
- ▮ Water Slide
- ▮ Food Stand
- 〜 Water
- 〜 Sidewalk

▲ A picture map can use shapes or symbols to show where things are.

The Key to Using Maps

The box at the bottom of a map is the **key**. Use the map key to learn the **meanings** of map symbols. Mapmakers use shapes to stand for real things. On the Street Map, what do the squares stand for?

Street Map

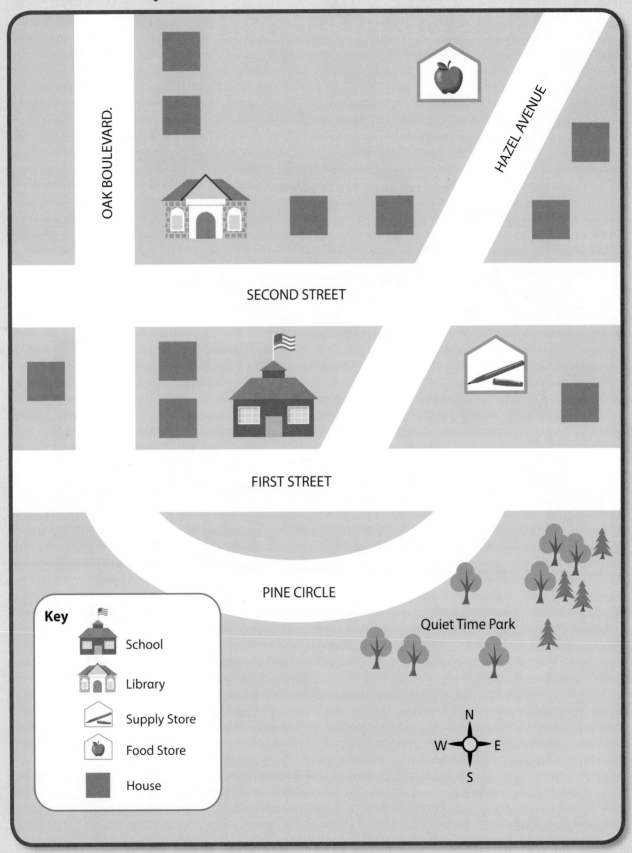

Key
- School
- Library
- Supply Store
- Food Store
- House

OAK BOULEVARD.

HAZEL AVENUE

SECOND STREET

FIRST STREET

PINE CIRCLE

Quiet Time Park

N
W ← → E
S

▲ A street map shows street names and symbols to help people find their way around town.

Symbols on the Road

Symbols on a road map help drivers find their way. A symbol shaped like a shield stands for a highway. Black circles stand for cities or towns.

Road Map

A road map shows where roads and cities are.

Rain or Shine: Weather Symbols

What will the weather be like tomorrow? Look at a weather map in your city's newspaper.

Symbols on the Weather Map show the weather. Use the key to understand what the symbols mean.

Weather Map

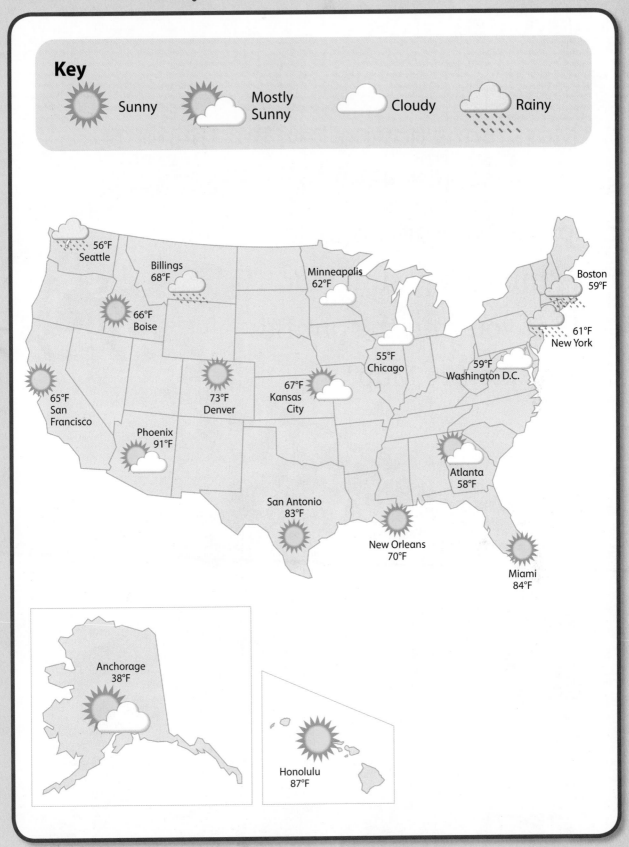

Key

Sunny

Mostly Sunny

Cloudy

Rainy

56°F Seattle

Billings 68°F

Minneapolis 62°F

Boston 59°F

66°F Boise

61°F New York

55°F Chicago

59°F Washington D.C.

65°F San Francisco

73°F Denver

67°F Kansas City

Phoenix 91°F

Atlanta 58°F

San Antonio 83°F

New Orleans 70°F

Miami 84°F

Anchorage 38°F

Honolulu 87°F

▲ A weather map shows what the weather is like all around the country.

No Key Needed: Picture Symbols

Most maps have a key. But there are some maps that don't have one. These maps use symbols that look like the real things they stand for.

Can you find the giraffes on this Picture Map?

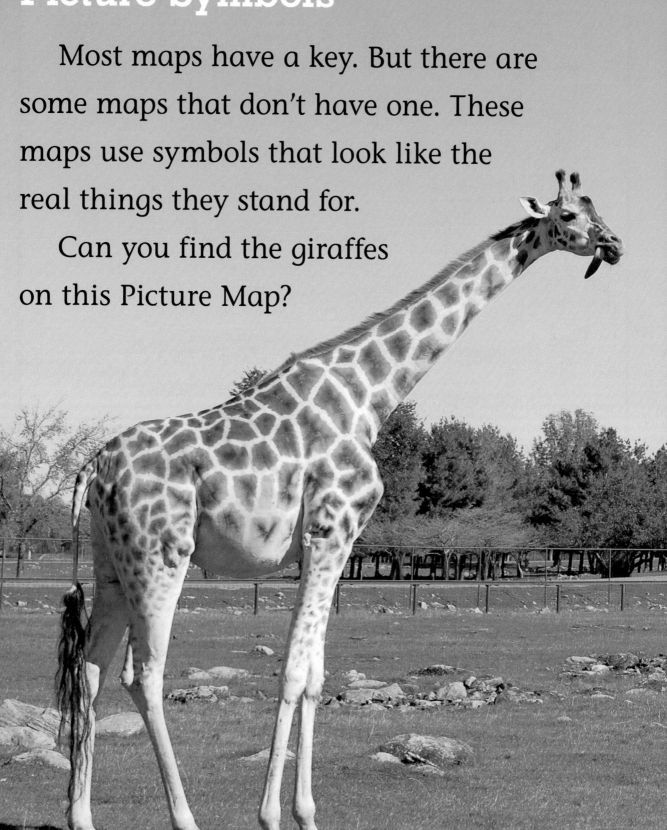

Picture Map

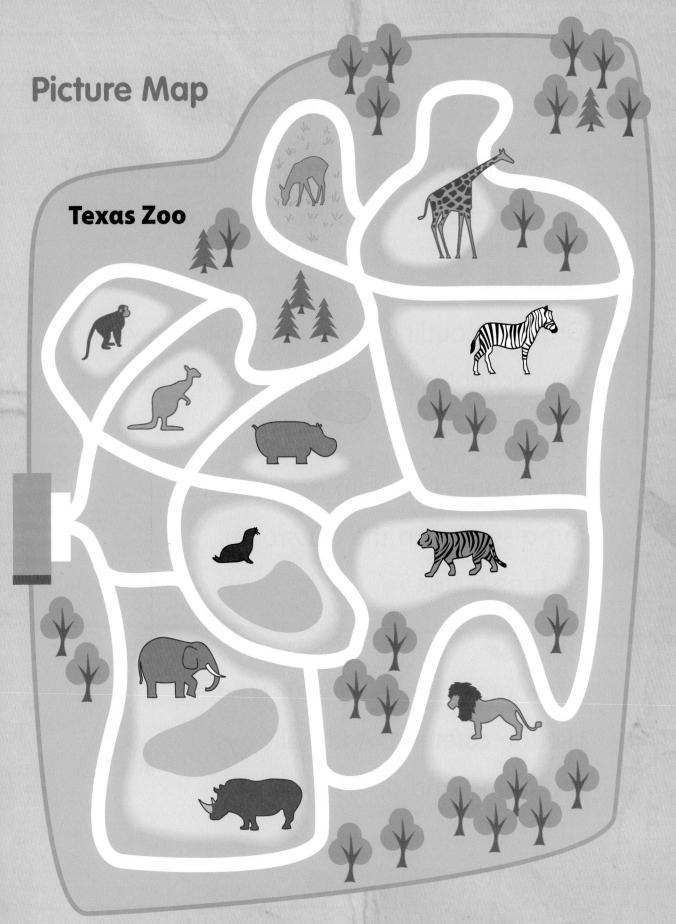

Texas Zoo

▲ This picture map uses picture symbols to show where to find the animals at the zoo.

Make Your Own Map

Use these steps to make your own map. Try to draw a map of your school.

Step 1

Draw the outline of your school. Show what your school would look like from above.

Step 2

Draw your classroom as a square. Put a symbol in the classroom, such as a star.

Step 3

Draw other rooms in your school, like the cafeteria. Add hallways, restrooms, and doors.

Step 4

Draw the library. Put a symbol in the library, such as an X.

Step 5

Make a key for your map. Draw and label the symbols for all the places you put on your map. ❖

Picture Map

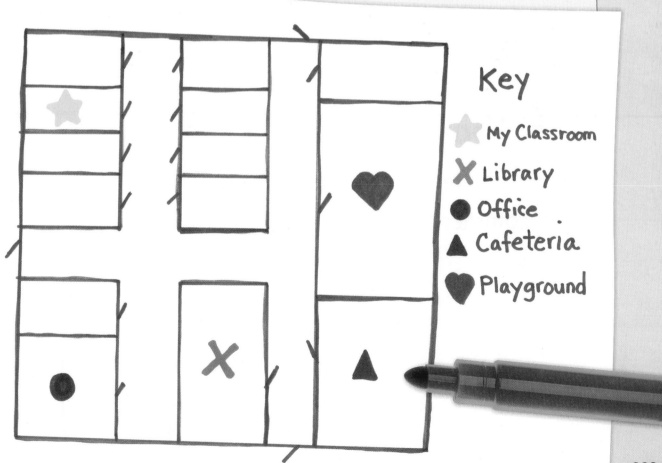

Key
★ My Classroom
✗ Library
● Office
▲ Cafeteria
♥ Playground

Talk About It

1. What does a **map** **key** **show**?

A map key shows ____ .

2. How is a weather map different than the other maps in the selection?

A weather map ____ . The other maps ____ .

3. Why do people use road maps?

People use road maps to ____ .

Learn test-taking strategies.
⊘ NGReach.com

Write About It

What did you learn from "If Maps Could Talk"?
Write a comment.

I learned ____ from page ____ .

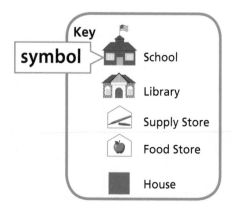

Use Information

What **signs** and symbols did you see in the text? What do they **mean**?

T Chart

Symbols and Signs	What It Means
	• mostly sunny • •

Use your chart. Tell a partner what you learned about signs, symbols, and maps.

A symbol can be a picture of a real thing.

Suffixes

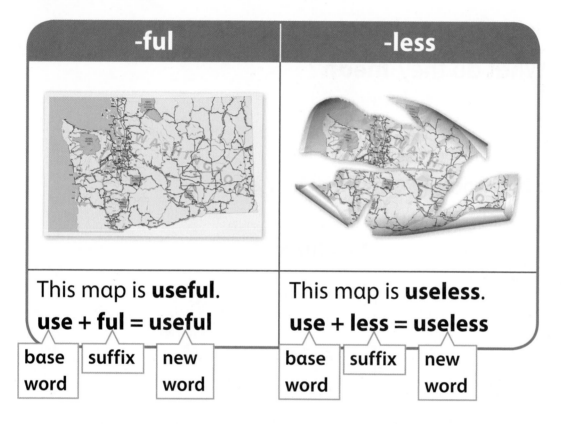

-ful	-less
This map is **useful**. use + ful = useful	This map is **useless**. use + less = useless

base word — suffix — new word

base word — suffix — new word

Sometimes you can add a **suffix**, like **–ful** or **–less**, to the end of a word to make a new word. What do **useful** and **useless** mean?

Try It Together

Add **-ful** and **-less** to each word. How do the meanings change?

Word	-ful	-less
care	careful	careless
help		
hope		

Connect Across Texts Read more about how **maps** and directions lead us to interesting places.

Genre A **poem** uses words to create images in your mind.

Haiku

By Richard Wright

Keep straight down this block
Then turn right where you will find
A peach tree blooming

Compare Genres

How are the words in "If Maps Could Talk" and "Haiku" different?

Informational Text

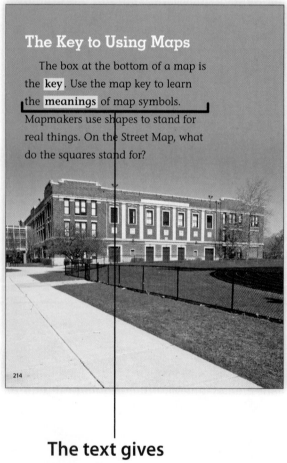

The Key to Using Maps

The box at the bottom of a map is the key. Use the map key to learn the meanings of map symbols. Mapmakers use shapes to stand for real things. On the Street Map, what do the squares stand for?

214

The text gives definitions.

Poem

Keep straight down this block
Then turn right where you will find
A peach tree blooming

228

The words create images in your mind.

Talk Together

Think about what you read and learned. Why do we need maps?

Adverbs

An **adverb** can tell more about a **verb**.

We **stand** **quietly** by the peach tree.

Grammar Rules Adverbs

Adverbs can tell:	Examples
• **how** something happens. These adverbs often end in -**ly**.	They **walk** **slowly**.
• **where** something happens.	The peach tree **is** **north** of the bench.
• **when** something happens.	We **always** **visit** the peach tree.

Read a Sentence

Which word is an adverb? How do you know?

The flower petals fall softly from the tree.

Write a Sentence

Write a sentence to tell how you got ready for school today. Use an adverb.

High Frequency Words

once

story

tell

Tell a Story

Listen and chant.   *Chant* (((**MP3**)))

Jack and the Hike

A story has a problem,
A solution as well.
Here is an example
Of a story to tell.

Once upon a time,
A boy named Jack.
Went on a hike
And lost his way back.

He looked to the east.
He looked to the west.
He looked for the path
That was the best.

He looked up and down,
And then . . . hooray!
He looked on a map
And found his way.

Key Words

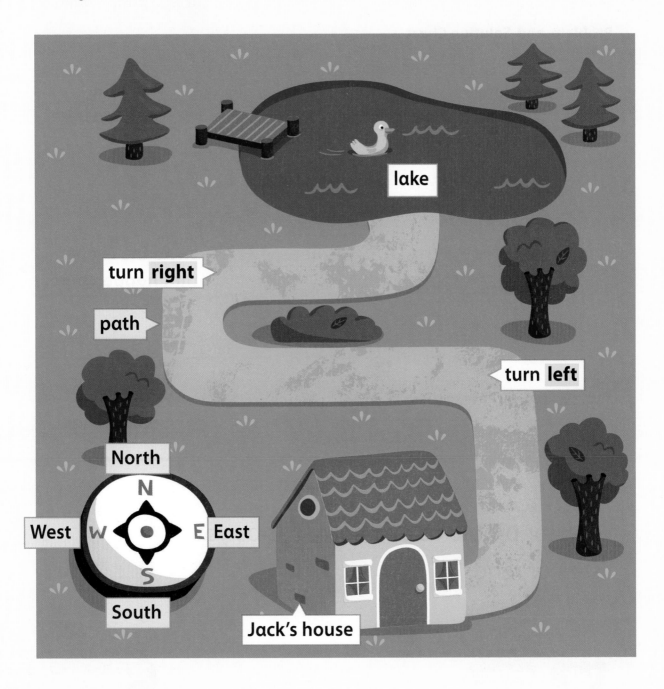

- lake
- turn **right**
- path
- turn **left**
- North
- West
- East
- South
- Jack's house

Talk Together

Use the map to tell a story.

Identify Problem and Solution

Problem-and-Solution Chart

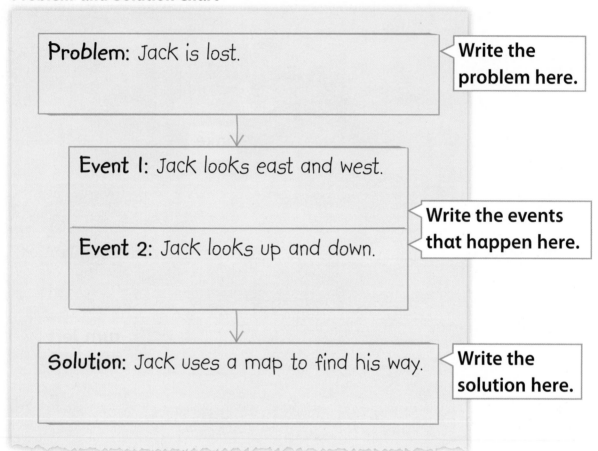

Problem: Jack is lost.

Write the problem here.

Event 1: Jack looks east and west.

Event 2: Jack looks up and down.

Write the events that happen here.

Solution: Jack uses a map to find his way.

Write the solution here.

Look for problems and solutions as you listen or read.

Talk Together

Tell a different story. Imagine Jack is with a friend. Make a problem-and-solution chart.

More Key Words

direction

North is a **direction**.

• far

The red states are **far** from each other.

• follow

path

Follow the path through the grass.

location

our tent

Our tent is in a good **location** by the lake.

• near

I sit **near** the window.

• High Frequency Word

Talk Together

Describe a **Key Word** while your partner asks questions about it.

There are four of them. One of them is South.

Is it direction?

Add words to My Vocabulary Notebook.
NGReach.com

Read a Modern Fairy Tale

A **modern fairy tale** is a new version of an old story that has been told for many years.

Most fairy tales begin like this.

Once upon a time, a young girl lived in a village south of a forest.

Reading Strategy

As you read, think of the 7 strategies you learned. Which strategies will help you understand the text?

Caperucita Roja

by **Argentina Palacios**

illustrated by **Valeria Docompo**

 Comprehension Coach

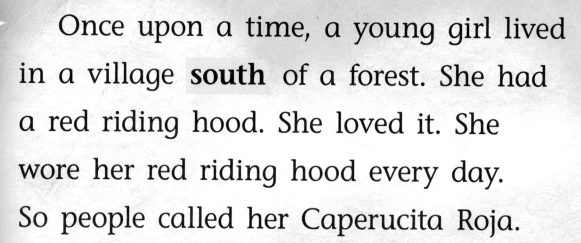

Once upon a time, a young girl lived in a village **south** of a forest. She had a red riding hood. She loved it. She wore her red riding hood every day. So people called her Caperucita Roja.

One day, Caperucita Roja's Mamá said,
"Hija, Abuelita is sick. Take her some food.
Visit with her for a while."

"Sí, Mamá," Caperucita Roja said.
"I will go now."

"**Follow** the shortest **path**. Do not get distracted. Go quickly!" Mamá said. "Do not forget your map."

"Sí, Mamá. I will take the map with me," said Caperucita Roja.

The village was south of the forest.
Abuelita's house was **north** of the forest.
Caperucita Roja followed the **directions**
on her map. She knew exactly where to go!

Abuelita's House

Farmer's House

Forest

Caperucita Roja's House

Village

N
W — E
S

0   10   15   20   25

Suddenly, a wolf stepped out of the forest. He was big, and he was bad. So people called him Big Bad Wolf.

"Hello, Caperucita Roja," he said. "Look at those pretty flowers. You should take some flowers to Abuelita."

One, two, three, four flowers. Caperucita
Roja got distracted.

The wolf wanted to eat Caperucita Roja.
But people were walking on the path.
They would not want Caperucita Roja to
be eaten. They would stop him.

Big Bad Wolf was unhappy. Then he had an idea.

He ran away, but Caperucita Roja didn't notice. She was too busy picking flowers for Abuelita.

Big Bad Wolf thought he could get to Abuelita's house before Caperucita Roja. He checked his map to see what path he could take.

He ran to the **west**. Then he ran to the north. Then he ran a little to the **east**.

ABUELITA'S HOUSE

FARMER'S HOUSE

FOREST

CAPERUCITA ROJA'S HOUSE

-LAGE

Big Bad Wolf knocked on Abuelita's door. "It is Caperucita Roja," he said.

"Come in, my dear," said Abuelita.

The wolf looked at Abuelita. He didn't want to eat her at all. She was too skinny.

"She does not look tasty," Big Bad Wolf said to himself. So he pushed Abuelita out of the bed and into the closet!

Then Big Bad Wolf put on one of Abuelita's nightgowns. "Now I look like Abuelita. I will eat Caperucita Roja," he said to himself.

Caperucita Roja knocked on the door.

"Come in!" Big Bad Wolf tried to sound like Abuelita. But his voice was too low.

"That does not sound like Abuelita," Caperucita Roja said to herself. She opened the door. Something was wrong.

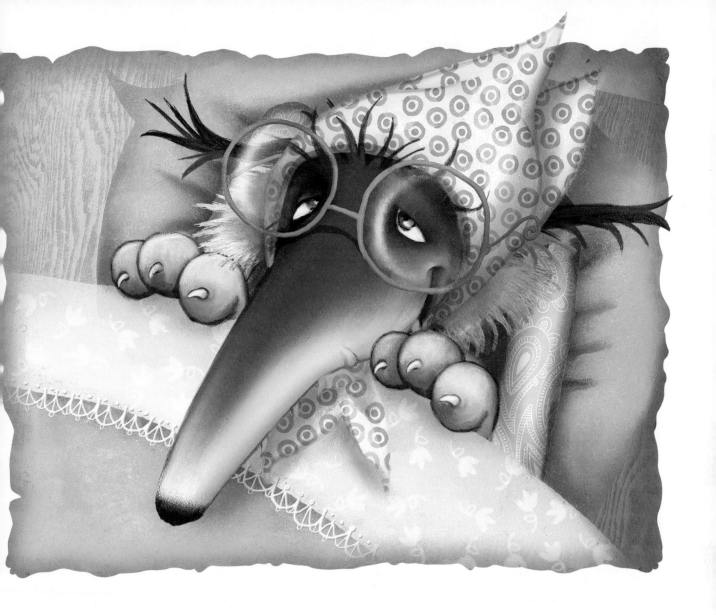

Caperucita Roja saw two long ears.

They were not Abuelita's ears.

Then she saw one very long nose.

It was not Abuelita's nose.

She saw two little, brown eyes.

They were not Abuelita's eyes.

Caperucita Roja thought fast. "Who can help me? The farmer can! I will go get the farmer!"

Caperucita Roja looked at her map. It showed where the farmer lived.

Abuelita's House

Farmer's House

N
W   E
S

0   5   10   15   20

Caperucita Roja went east. She ran and ran. She told the farmer about the wolf.

"I scare rabbits out of my garden every day. I will scare away that wolf! I will save Abuelita!" he shouted. And they ran off together.

When Big Bad Wolf saw the angry
farmer, he jumped out of the bed. He
tried to go **right**. He tried to go **left**.
He could not escape. The farmer was
too fast for him. So Big Bad Wolf
jumped out of the window!

Caperucita Roja opened the closet door.
She helped Abuelita back into the bed.

"Thank you for your help!" Caperucita
Roja said to the farmer. "I could not have
saved Abuelita without you."

Abuelita began to feel better quickly. She and the farmer became good friends. They never saw Big Bad Wolf again.

Caperucita Roja often came to visit Abuelita and the farmer. And they all lived happily ever after. ❖

Meet the Author

Argentina Palacios

AWARD WINNER

Argentina Palacios was born in Panama, and then moved to the United States. She was a Spanish teacher in Texas.

Now Ms. Palacios writes stories in English and Spanish. She also gives tours to children at a zoo because she loves animals.

◄ **Argentina Palacios**

Writer's Craft

Argentina Palacios ended this story by solving the problem and telling us what happens to the characters afterward. What else would you add to the ending?

Talk About It

1. Which character in the story is sick?

_____ is sick.

2. How does Big Bad Wolf get to Abuelita's house before Caperucita Roja?

Big Bad Wolf _____ .

3. How does Caperucita Roja use a map to get help?

Caperucita Roja uses a map to _____ .

Learn test-taking strategies.
⊘ NGReach.com

Write About It

This fairy tale teaches you to know when you are in trouble and to go for help. When have you needed help? Who did you go to?

I needed help _____ .
I went to _____ .

Identify Problem and Solution

Caperucita Roja has a problem with the Big Bad Wolf. What is it and how does she solve it?

Problem-and-Solution Chart

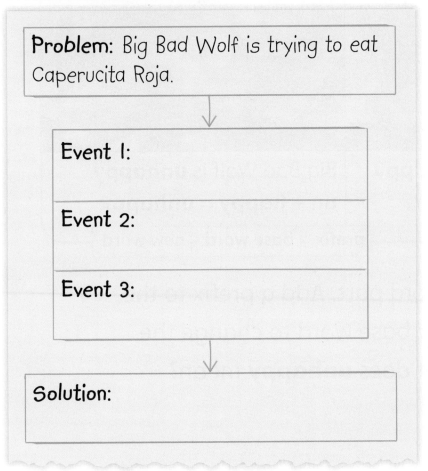

Problem: Big Bad Wolf is trying to eat Caperucita Roja.

↓

Event 1:

Event 2:

Event 3:

↓

Solution:

Use your chart to retell the story of *Caperucita Roja*.

The farmer scares Big Bad Wolf away.

Prefixes

base word	un-
Caperucita is **happy**.	Big Bad Wolf is **unhappy**.
happy	**un + happy = unhappy**
base word	prefix · base word · new word

A **prefix** is a word part. Add a prefix to the **beginning** of a base word to change the meaning. What does **unhappy** mean?

Try It Together

Add the prefix **un-** to each word. Talk about the new meaning of each word.

Word	New Word
lucky	unlucky
safe	
kind	
fair	

NATIONAL
GEOGRAPHIC
EXCLUSIVE

Connect Across Texts Learn more about what helps us use maps.

Genre A **how-to article** teaches you how to do something.

How to Make a Compass

by Michael A. DiSpezio

A compass is a tool that can tell which **direction** you are going. There are four main directions: **North**, **South**, **East**, and **West**.

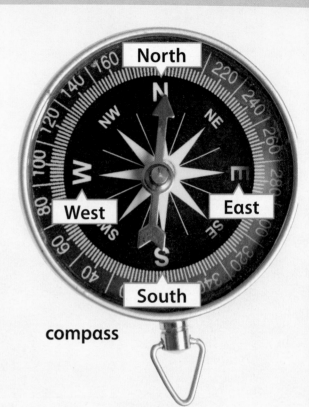

compass

Materials

sewing needle

clear container

water

bar magnet

plastic foam cup

paper

crayons

scissors

Step 1

Cut out the bottom of the foam cup so you have a flat circle.

Step 2

Magnetize the needle. Rub it the same direction on the bar magnet 20 times.

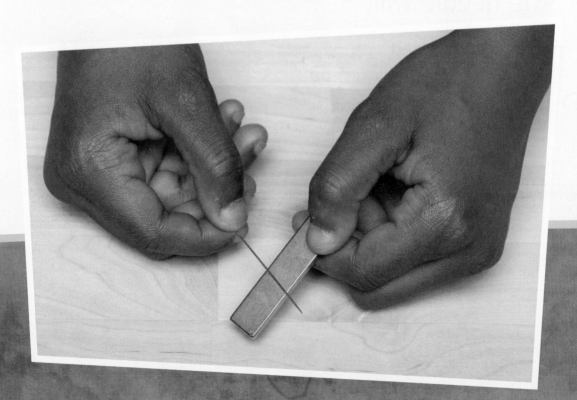

Step 3

Lay the needle on the foam circle.

Step 4

Put the foam and the needle in the water. The needle will stop moving when it points North.

Step 5

Draw a compass rose like this one.

Fill the clear container with water. Place it over your compass rose.

Step 6

Move the paper around until the needle lines up with the N on the compass rose.

Think of all the places north of you. Which places are south of you?

Compare Genres

How are the purposes of a fairy tale like *Caperucita Roja* and a How-to Article like "How to Make a Compass" different?

Fairy Tale

Suddenly, a wolf stepped out of the forest. He was big, and he was bad. So people called him Big Bad Wolf.

"Hello, Caperucita Roja," he said. "Look at those pretty flowers. You should take some flowers to Abuelita."

243

Tells a story that cannot happen in real life.

How-to Article

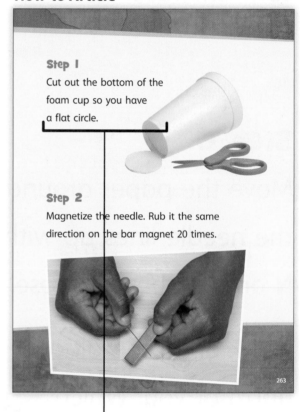

Step 1
Cut out the bottom of the foam cup so you have a flat circle.

Step 2
Magnetize the needle. Rub it the same direction on the bar magnet 20 times.

263

Tells how to make something that is real.

Talk Together

Think about what you read and learned. Why do we need maps?

Prepositions

Prepositions tell where something is.

The needle is **on** the foam.

The compass is **next to** the map.

Grammar Rules Prepositions

Prepositions tell where. Put prepositions before the noun that names a place.	The compass is **on** the **table**.
	preposition ⟶ / noun that names a place

Read a Sentence

Draw what the sentence tells. Use your drawing to tell a partner what the preposition means.

The compass rose is **under** the glass.

Write a Sentence

Write a sentence that tells where you find scissors in your classroom. Use a preposition. Read it to a partner.

Write as a Reader

Write Literary Response ✏️

Think about a story. What was the problem and solution? What did you like about it? Write a response for a partner.

Caperucita Roja

by Aziza Noor

I read Caperucita Roja. **Caperucita Roja**

problem ▷ **had to save Abuelita from the wolf**.

Caperucita Roja ran to get the farmer.

solution ▷ **The helpful farmer scared the wolf away.**

They all lived happily ever after. I think this happy ending makes Caperucita Roja a good story.

Tell the title of the story.

Tell what the story is about.

Tell what you liked about the story.

1 Plan and Write

Talk with a partner about stories you have read. Pick one story you like. Talk about how the author tells the story. Tell your partner the story's problem and solution.

Write the problem and solution. Then write what makes the story good.

2 Check Your Work

Revise and edit your writing. Use this checklist.

Checklist

☑ Does the story you reviewed have a strong ending?

☑ Can you add any prefixes or suffixes?

☑ Check your sentences. Did you use prepositions correctly?

☑ Check for different ways to spell sounds you know. Circle words to check. Correct spelling errors.

3 Finish and Share

Finish your response. Write each sentence neatly. Begin a new paragraph when you change ideas.

Read your response clearly. Listen carefully to your partner. Then ask questions. Share what you know.

Why was the ending your favorite part of Caperucita Roja?

Share Your Ideas

Think about what maps show us. Why do we need maps? Choose one of these ways to share your ideas about the **Big Question**.

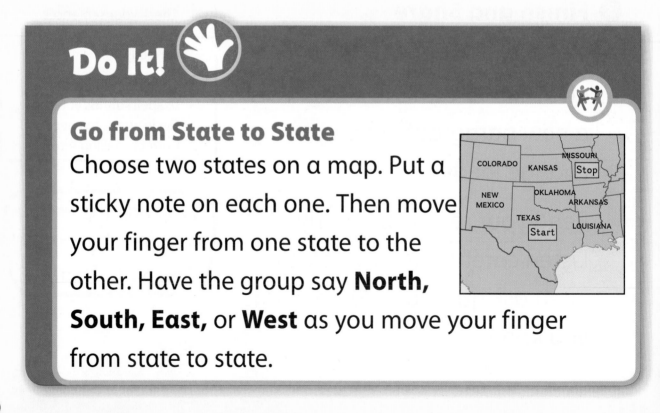

Do It!

Go from State to State

Choose two states on a map. Put a sticky note on each one. Then move your finger from one state to the other. Have the group say **North, South, East,** or **West** as you move your finger from state to state.

Talk About It!

Give Directions

Hide an object, such as a crayon. Then give good directions so that your partner can find the object. Take turns.

Go to the plants near the window. Look between the books.

Write It!

Draw a Map

Draw a map of your neighborhood. Use symbols in your map. Draw a map key that shows what the symbols stand for.

My Neighborhood

Spring Street

Key
■ House
▲ Park

a
b
c
d
e
f
g
h
i
j
k
l
m
n
o
p
q
r
s
t
u
v
w
x
y
z

A

alike

*These cats look **alike**.*

B

back

*The **back** tire is flat.*

beak

*This bird's **beak** is colorful.*

better

*Martha got a **better** grade.*

between

*The house is **between** the two trees.*

blow

*The wind will **blow** the tree down.*

body

*A baby has a small **body**.*

build

*You can **build** things with blocks.*

C

calendar

*This **calendar** shows the month of December.*

climb

*Orangutans can **climb** trees.*

cloudy

*It is a **cloudy** day.*

cold

*The snow is **cold**.*

a
b
c
d
e
f
g
h
i
j
k
l
m
n
o
p
q
r
s
t
u
v
w
x
y
z

communicate

*People **communicate** by talking and writing.*

computer

*Jim does work on a **computer**.*

cool

*The fan keeps me **cool**.*

corner

Ashley Miller

*I write my name in the **corner** of the paper.*

coverings

feathers

shell

*Birds and turtles have different **coverings**.*

different

*These fruits are **different**.*

direction

*North is a **direction**.*

distance

*This man runs a long **distance**.*

easier

*It is **easier** to carry the books one at a time.*

east (East)

*New York is on the **east** coast of the United States.*

fact

*It's a **fact** that a dog has four legs.*

a
b
c
d
e
f
g
h
i
j
k
l
m
n
o
p
q
r
s
t
u
v
w
x
y
z

far

*The orange states are **far** from each other.*

fast

*This car is going **fast**.*

feathers

*This eagle's **feathers** help it to fly.*

feature

*A long neck is the main **feature** of a giraffe.*

feel

*The rabbit's fur **feels** soft.*

fly

*The gulls **fly** together.*

follow

path

Follow the path through the grass.

front

The **front** of the house is blue.

fur

This big dog has a lot of **fur**.

future

past   present   future

kindergarden   first grade   second grade

In the **future** I will be in second grade.

H

history

Study **history** to learn what happened long ago.

hot

Do not touch! The stove is **hot**.

a b c d e **f g h** i j k l m n o p q r s t u v w x y z

a
b
c
d
e
f
g
h
i
j
k
l
m
n
o
p
q
r
s
t
u
v
w
x
y
z

I

Internet

Sarah reads good news on the **Internet**.

invent

People **invent** *things like the telephone.*

K

key

A map **key** *uses symbols to show where things are.*

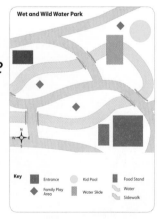

L

left

Turn **left** *when you see this sign.*

location

Our tent is in a good **location** *by the lake.*

look

These apples **look** *the same.*

machine

This **machine** washes dishes.

map

This **map** shows where they are.

meaning

The dictionary shows us the **meaning** of words.

message

Jane got a text **message**.

modern

The cell phone is more **modern** than the old phone.

month

Our favorite **month** is July.

mouth

*This crocodile has a large **mouth**.*

movement

*The **movement** of a tortoise is slow.*

music

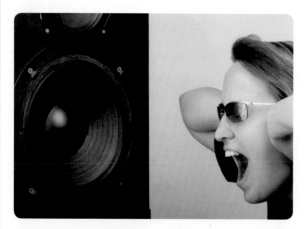

*This **music** is very loud.*

near

*I sit **near** the window.*

new

*This family has a **new** baby.*

news

*He is watching the **news** on TV.*

north (North)

*Nebraska is **north** of Texas.*

now

*The test starts right **now**.*

O

old

*This car is very **old**.*

outside

*They play **outside**.*

P

parts

*This engine has many **parts**.*

past

past	present	future
kindergarden	first grade	second grade

*In the **past** I was in kindergarten.*

a
b
c
d
e
f
g
h
i
j
k
l
m
n
o
p
q
r
s
t
u
v
w
x
y
z

path

This **path** goes through the woods.

paw

This is a cat's **paw**.

picture

These **pictures** sit on a desk.

power

This toaster uses **power**.

present

past	present	future
kindergarden	first grade	second grade

Today is the **present**. I am in first grade.

push

We had to **push** the car.

R

rainy

*It is a **rainy** day.*

record

*This old **record** has some fun music.*

right

*Turn **right** when you see this sign.*

run

*We like to **run** during recess.*

S

scales

*The **scales** on this snake are beautiful.*

show

*I **show** my drawing.*

a
b
c
d
e
f
g
h
i
j
k
l
m
n
o
p
q
r
s
t
u
v
w
x
y
z

a
b
c
d
e
f
g
h
i
j
k
l
m
n
o
p
q
r
s
t
u
v
w
x
y
z

sign

This **sign** means to add.

slide

We like to **slide** at the park.

slither

The snake **slithers** across the ground.

snowy

This mountain is very **snowy**.

soft

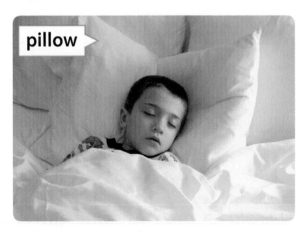

pillow

Pillows are **soft**.

south (South)

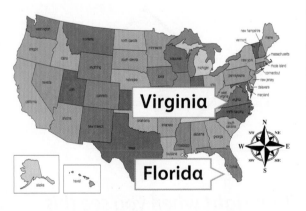

Virginia

Florida

Florida is **south** of Virginia.

storm

*Our family stays inside when there is a **storm**.*

strong

*We are **strong**.*

sunny

*It is a **sunny** day.*

swim

*We like to **swim** in the pool.*

symbol

*This flag is a **symbol** of America.*

T

tail

*This lemur has a long **tail**.*

temperature

*It's cold! The **temperature** is only 8° Fahrenheit.*

then

*Back **then**, I didn't know how to walk.*

tool

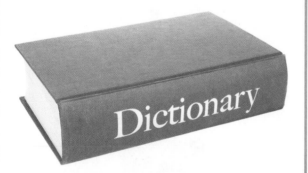

*A dictionary is a **tool** you can use to look up words.*

U

useful

*This hammer is very **useful**.*

W

warm

*The blanket keeps us **warm**.*

weather

*We like the warm **weather**.*

west (West)

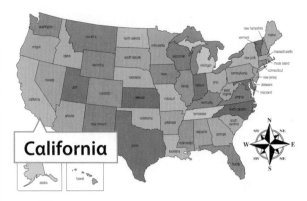

California

*California is on the **west** coast of the United States.*

wind

*The **wind** is very strong today.*

Y

year

*This has been a fun **year**.*

a
b
c
d
e
f
g
h
i
j
k
l
m
n
o
p
q
r
s
t
u
v
w
x
y
z

Index

A

Academic vocabulary 7, 43, 75, 107, 143, 175, 209, 235

Activate prior knowledge 2, 71, 76, 139, 205

Adverbs 231

Alligators 33-37, 38, 39

Alphabetizing 164, **192**, **202**

Animals 2, 3, 4, 5, 6, 38, 40, 41, 42, 45-57, 58, 59, 60, 61-63, 64, 66, 67, 68, 69

Animal fantasy 8

Antonyms 60, 201

Ask questions
about stories 8, 210, 236
about other texts 209
types
literal 69, 133
open-ended 8, 69, 133

Author's style 29, 125, 189, 257

B

Build Background 2, 71, 139, 205

C

Capital letters 39

Categorizing 42, 59

Cause and effect 74, **95**, 135

Chant 4, 40, 232

Characters,
actions 30, 31, **102**, 125, 126, 174, 189, 190, 191, 258, 259
compare 31
feelings 108, 126, **174**, **176**, 189, 190, **191**
motivations 30, 102, 126, 190

story **8**, 29, 30, 31, 102, 108, 125, 126, 132, 174, 176, 189, 190, 191, 257, 258, 259
traits 29, 30, 31, 258

Classify 106, **127**

Communication 140, 141, 142, 143, 145-161, 162, 163

Compare
genres **38**, **64**, **132**, **170**, **198**, **230**, **266**
texts 33, 38, 44, 58, 61, 64, 97, 129, 132, 165, 170, 193, 198, 227, 261

Compare and contrast 4, 5, **6**, 30, **31**, 33, 38, 42, 64, 132, 141, 162, 163, 170, 193, 198, 230, 266

Compass 261-265

Complete Sentences 39

Compound words 96, **128**, 135, 201

Connections, making
text to own experiences **8**, 30, 190, 198, 210, 236, 266
text to text **33**, **38**, **44**, 58, **61**, 64, **97**, **129**, 132, **165**, 170, **193**, 198, 210, 236, **227**, **261**
text to larger community **44**, 198, 210, 236

Content Vocabulary
see Vocabulary

Context clues, using to determine
meanings 201
unfamiliar words 201

Conventions, in writing
capitalization
for months and days of week 201
for proper nouns 201
for salutation and closing of letter 201
to begin sentences 39

Acknowledgments, continued

Text Credits

Unit Five

Houghton Mifflin Harcourt: *For Pete's Sake* by Ellen Stoll Walsh. Copyright © 1998 by Ellen Stoll Walsh. Reprinted by permission of Houghton Mifflin Harcourt Publishing Company. All rights reserved.

School Specialty Publishing: Excerpt from *Slither, Slide, Hop and Run* by Katharine Kenah. Text copyright © 2006 by School Specialty Publishing. Reprinted by permission of School Specialty Publishing.

Unit Six

HarperCollins Publishers: Excerpt from *I Face the Wind* by Vicki Cobb, illustrated by Julia Gorton. Copyright © 2003 by Vicki Cobb. Illustrations copyright © 2003 by Julia Gorton. Reprinted by permission of HarperCollins Publishers.

Houghton Mifflin Harcourt: Excerpt from *A Year for Kiko* by Ferida Wolff, illustrated by Joung Un Kim. Text copyright © 1997 by Ferida Wolff. Illustrations © 1997 by Joung Un Kim. Text reprinted by permission of the author. Illustrations used by permission of Houghton Mifflin Harcourt Publishing Company. All rights reserved.

Unit Seven

Lerner Publishing Group, Inc.: Excerpt from *Communication Then and Now* by Robin Nelson. Copyright © 2003 by Lerner Publishing Group, Inc. Reprinted by permission of Lerner Publications Company, a division of Lerner Publishing Group, Inc. All rights reserved. No part of this text excerpt may be used or reproduced in any manner whatsoever without the prior written permission of Lerner Publishing Group, Inc.

Little, Brown and Company: Excerpt from "Vacuum Cleaner," from *Imaginative Inventions* by Charise Mericle Harper. Copyright © 2001 by Charise Mericle Harper. Reprinted by permission of Little, Brown and Company. All rights reserved.

Unit Eight

Capstone Press: Excerpt from *If Maps Could Talk* by Erika L. Shores. Copyright © 2008 by Capstone Press. Reprinted by permission of Capstone Press. All rights reserved.

Arcade Publishing: "Keep straight down this block," by Richard Wright, from *Haiku: This Other World*. Copyright © 1998 by Ellen Wright. Published by Arcade Publishing, New York, New York. Reprinted by permission of the publisher.

☐ **NATIONAL GEOGRAPHIC SCHOOL PUBLISHING**

National Geographic School Publishing gratefully acknowledges the contributions of the following National Geographic Explorers to our program and to our planet:

Josh Thorne, 2008 National Geographic Emerging Explorer
Michael Fay, National Geographic Explorer-in-Residence
Cid Simoes and Paola Segura, 2008 National Geographic Emerging Explorers
Mariana Fuentes, National Geographic Grantee
Greg Marshall, National Geographic Scientist
Tim Samaras, 2005 National Geographic Emerging Explorer
Constance Adams, 2005 National Geographic Emerging Explorer
Michael DiSpezio, National Geographic Presenter

Photographic Credits

iv (tl) Kevin Schafer/Alamy Images. v (tc) Carsten Peter/National Geographic Image Collection. vi (tl) Museum of the City of New York/Corbis. vii (tc) Corbis Premium RF/Alamy Images. ix (tr) Corbis Premium RF/Alamy Images. 2-3 (bg) Arco Images GmbH/Alamy Images. 3 (inset) Liz Garza Williams/Hampton-Brown/National Geographic School Publishing. 5 (bl) PhotoDisc/Getty Images. (br) PhotoDisc/Getty Images. (cl) Eric Isselée/iStockphoto. (cr) Eric Isselée/Shutterstock. (tl) NatUlrich/Shutterstock. (tr) Michael Lynch/Alamy Images. 6 (bl) DigitalStock/Corbis. (br) Brand X Pictures/Jupiterimages. (tl) Jello5700/iStockphoto. (tr) Edwin Verin/Shutterstock. 7 (bc) Artville. (bl) Michele Burgess/Corbis. (br) Artville. (tcl) Rosemarie Gearhart/iStockphoto. (tcr) Artville. (tl) Alan Carey/Corbis. (tr) PhotoDisc/Getty Images. 30 MBI/Alamy Images. 31 teve Snowden/iStockphoto. 33 Heidi and Hans-Jurgen Koch/Minden Pictures/National Geographic Image Collection. 34 Otis Imboden/National Geographic Image Collection. 35 Kevin Schafer/Alamy Images. 36-37 John Zellmer/iStockphoto. 38 Kevin Schafer/Alamy Images. 39 PhotoDisc/Getty Images. 40 Ljupco/iStockphoto. 41 (bl) Corbis/Jupiterimages. (br) Frans Lemmens/Corbis. (cl) Dan Guravich/Corbis. (cr) Luiz Claudio Marigo/Nature Picture Library. (tl) John Foxx Images/Imagestate. (tr) Creatas/Jupiterimages. 42 (l) Abramova Kseniya/Shutterstock. (r) Andreas Weiss/Shutterstock. 43 (bl) age fotostock/SuperStock. (br) PE Forsberg/Alamy Images. (tc) Anna Sedneva/Shutterstock. (tl) Nick Kirk/Alamy Images. (tr) colin streater/Alamy Images. 44 (inset) Frank Leung/iStockphoto. 44-45 (bg) Rich Lindie/Shutterstock. 46 (b) Paul Tessier/iStockphoto. (t) Frank Leung/iStockphoto. 47 (b) Paul Chesley/Getty Images. (t) Fivespots/Shutterstock. 48 (b) John Carnemolla/Shutterstock. (t) Eric Isselée/iStockphoto. 49 Alexia Khruscheva/Shutterstock. 50 (b) Matt Abbe/iStockphoto. (t) pkruger/iStockphoto. 51 EcoPrint/Shutterstock. 52 Eric Isselée/iStockphoto. 53 Wojciech Jaskowski/Shutterstock. 54 H Lansdown/Alamy Images. 55 Edd Westmacott/Alamy Images. 56 (b) Ron Heijman/iStockphoto. (t) Eric Isselée/iStockphoto. 57 (b) Ingram Publishing/Superstock. (t) Wayne Tam/iStockphoto. 59 Michael DeLeon/iStockphoto. 60 (l) Eric Isselée/Shutterstock. (r) pkruger/iStockphoto. 61 (bg) Hampton-Brown/National Geographic School Publishing. (l) National Geographic Image Collection. (r) EuToch/iStockphoto. 62 (b) Dr. Michael Heithaus. (t) Mark Mallchok/Brella Productions. 62-63 (bg) Hampton-Brown/National Geographic School Publishing. 63 (b) Greg Marshall/National Geographic Image Collection. (t) National Geographic Image Collection. 64 (bl) Matt Abbe/iStockphoto. (br) Dr. Michael Heithaus. (rbg) Hampton-Brown/National Geographic School Publishing. (tl) pkruger/iStockphoto. (tr) Mark Mallchok/Brella Productions. 65 (bl) Stefan Klein/iStockphoto. (t) Stefan Klein/iStockphoto. 66 John Zellmer/iStockphoto. 68 Arco Images GmbH/Alamy Images. 69 (l) Blend Images/SuperStock. (r) Blend Images/SuperStock. 70-71 (bg) Warren Faidley/Corbis. 71 (inset) Liz Garza Williams/Hampton-Brown/National Geographic School Publishing. 73 (bl) Michael Rolands/iStockphoto. (br) ND1939/iStockphoto. (tl) Zastol`skiy Victor Leonidovich/Shutterstock. (tr) cristovao/Shutterstock. 74 Corbis/Jupiterimages. 75 (bl) Nicholas Eveleigh/Alamy Images. (br) Jim Arbogast/Digital Vision/Jupiterimages. (tc) Polka Dot Images/Jupiterimages. (tl) David Madison/Digital Vision/Jupiterimages. (tr) Design Pics/Jupiterimages. 95 (l) Nicole S. Young/iStockphoto. (r) Sean Locke/iStockphoto. 105 (bl) Antonio Jorge Nunes/iStockphoto. (br) sebos/iStockphoto. (cr) Sam Abell/National Geographic Image Collection.

(tl) Image Source. (tr) Randy Faris/Corbis. 106 Digital Vision/Getty Images. 107 (bl) Skip O'Donnell/iStockphoto. (tc) Nick Kennedy/Alamy Images. (tl) George F. Mobley/National Geographic Image Collection. (tr) David Chasey/Photodisc/Jupiterimages. (tr) David Hardman/iStockphoto. 125 Michael Wolff. 127 Blend Images/Alamy Images. 129 Carsten Peter/National Geographic Image Collection. 130 (b) Warren Faidley/Corbis. (c) Mark Thiessen/National Geographic Image Collection. (t) Hampton-Brown/National Geographic School Publishing. 130-131 (bg) Carsten Peter/National Geographic Image Collection. 132 Carsten Peter/National Geographic Image Collection. 133 (b) PhotoDisc/Getty Images. (t) Mark Thiessen/National Geographic Image Collection. 136 Warren Faidley/Corbis. 137 (b) Rick Holcomb/Hampton-Brown/National Geographic School Publishing. (t) Jose Luis Pelaez Inc/Blend Images/Jupiterimages. 138 (inset) Brasil2/iStockphoto. 138-139 (bg) Jupiterimages/Getty Images. 139 (inset) Getty Images/Jupiterimages. 141 (bl) George Marks/Getty Images. (br) Image Source/Alamy Images. (cl) George Marks/Getty Images. (cr) Pali Rao/iStockphoto. (tl) George Marks/Getty Images. (tr) Nina Shannon/iStockphoto. 142 MIXA/Alamy Images. 143 (l) PhotoAlto/Alamy Images. (r) Bettmann/Corbis. 144 (bl) North Wind Picture Archives. (br) SSPL/The Image Works, Inc. (tc) Oxford Science Archive / Heritage-Images/The Image Works, Inc. (tl) SSPL/The Image Works, Inc. (tr) SSPL/The Image Works, Inc. 145 (b) Fancy/Alamy Images. (t) Minnesota Historical Society/Corbis. 146-147 CRG Studios/Blend Images/Jupiterimages. 148 Pierre Vauthey/Corbis Sygma. 149 Michael Newman/PhotoEdit. 150 (b) Emilia Stasiak/Shutterstock. (t) The Granger Collection, New York. 151 (b) Photosani/Shutterstock. (t) Lester Lefkowitz/Taxi/Getty Images. 152 (b) Adrio Communications Ltd/Shutterstock. (t) Bettmann/Corbis. 153 (bg) BananaStock/Jupiterimages. (inset) Bettmann/Corbis. 154 (b) cyphix-photo/Shutterstock. (t) SuperStock. 155 (b) Elly Godfroy/Alamy Images. (t) Image Source/Corbis. 156 (bg) Museum of the City of New York/Corbis. (inset) Old Paper Studios/Alamy Images. 157 (b) Sean Locke/iStockphoto. (t) David Young-Wolff/PhotoEdit. 158 FPG/Getty Images. 160 (bl) North Wind Picture Archives. (br) SSPL/The Image Works, Inc. (tl) SSPL/The Image Works, Inc. (tr) Oxford Science Archive / Heritage-Images/The Image Works, Inc. 161 (bl) Topham/The Image Works, Inc. (br) michael ledray/Shutterstock. (tl) SSPL/The Image Works, Inc. (tr) SSPL/The Image Works, Inc. 162 (l) Liz Garza Williams/Hampton-Brown/National Geographic School Publishing. (r) PhotoDisc/Getty Images. 163 (l) Donna Coleman/iStockphoto. (r) Sean Locke/iStockphoto. 164 (l) Rob Marmion/Shutterstock. (r) Christophe Testi/Alamy Images. 165 (bg) PhotoDisc/Getty Images. (c) Mark Thiessen/Hampton-Brown/National Geographic School Publishing. (inset) NASA Human Space Flight Gallery. 166 (inset) NASA - GRIN (Great Images in NASA). 166-167 (bg) PhotoDisc/Getty Images. 167 (b) PhotoDisc/Getty Images. (t) NASA Human Space Flight Gallery. 168 (inset) NASA Human Space Flight Gallery. 168-169 (bg) PhotoDisc/Getty Images. 169 (inset) NASA Human Space Flight Gallery. 174 Liz Garza Williams/Hampton-Brown/National Geographic School Publishing. 175 (bc) Image Club. (bl) Sergey Peterman/Shutterstock. (br) Sebastian Crocker/Shutterstock. (tc) Holly Kuchera/Shutterstock. (tl) Asia Images Group Pte Ltd/Alamy Images. (tr) Irina Fischer/Shutterstock. 189 Chuku Lee/Pat Cummings. 190 (bc) Sibrikov Valery/Shutterstock. (bl) ajt/Shutterstock. (c) Elena Elisseeva/Shutterstock. (r) Kamyshko/Shutterstock. 192 (l) JGI/Jamie Grill/Jupiterimages. (r) Bozena/Shutterstock. 200 FPG/Getty Images. 201 Liz Garza Williams/Hampton-Brown/National

Geographic School Publishing. 202 (bg) Jupiterimages/Getty Images. (inset) Brasil2/iStockphoto. 203 (b) Yulli/Shutterstock. (t) Liz Garza Williams/Hampton-Brown/National Geographic School Publishing. 204 (inset) Liz Garza Williams/Hampton-Brown/National Geographic School Publishing. 204-205 (bg) Alaska Stock Images/age fotostock. 207 (cr) Michael Mattner/iStockphoto. 209 (bl) GlowImages/Alamy Images. (tl) Domenico Pellegriti/iStockphoto. (tr) PhotoDisc/Getty Images. 210-211 (bg) Sharon Day/Shutterstock. 211 (inset) Corbis Premium RF/Alamy Images. 212 eldirector77/Shutterstock. 213 Sharon Day/Shutterstock. 214 Steve Geer/iStockphoto. 215 Sharon Day/Shutterstock. 216 Chad McDermott/Shutterstock. 217 (bg) Sharon Day/Shutterstock. (inset) Fotocrisis/Shutterstock. 218 mihalec/Shutterstock. 219 Sharon Day/Shutterstock. 220 Sonja Fagnan/iStockphoto. 221 Sharon Day/Shutterstock. 222-223 (bg) Sharon Day/Shutterstock. (inset) STILLFX/Shutterstock. 225 indeed/Jupiterimages. 226 (l) Stacey Lynn Payne/Shutterstock. (r) Stacey Lynn Payne/Shutterstock. 235 (bl) Ben Blankenburg/iStockphoto. (br) Corbis. (tl) Tischenko Irina/Shutterstock. (tr) Diane N. Ennis/Shutterstock. 257 Claire Deroche/Argentina Palacios. 259 Liz Garza Williams/Hampton-Brown/National Geographic School Publishing. 261 (bg) Clearviewstock/Alamy Images. (inset) Eyecandy Images/Alamy Images. 262 (bcl, bl, c, tlc) Mark Thiessen/Hampton-Brown/National Geographic School Publishing. (tl) rusm/iStockphoto. (tr) Morgan Lane Photography/Shutterstock. 262-263 (bg) Clearviewstock/Alamy Images. 263 (b, t) Mark Thiessen/Hampton-Brown/National Geographic School Publishing. 264 (b, t) Mark Thiessen/Hampton-Brown/National Geographic School Publishing. 264-265 (bg) Clearviewstock/Alamy Images. 265 (b,t) Mark Thiessen/Hampton-Brown/National Geographic School Publishing. 266 (b, t) Mark Thiessen/Hampton-Brown/National Geographic School Publishing. (bg) Clearviewstock/Alamy Images. (t) Mark Thiessen/Hampton-Brown/National Geographic School Publishing. 267 Mark Thiessen/Hampton-Brown/National Geographic School Publishing. 270 Alaska Stock Images/age fotostock. 271 kate_sept2004/iStockphoto. 296 (bl) John Foxx Images/Imagestate. (br) photobank. kiev.ua/Shutterstock. (cl) Nick Kirk/Alamy Images. (cr) Domenico Pellegriti/iStockphoto. (tl) Alan Carey/Corbis. (tr) Jon Feingersh/Getty Images. 297 (bl) Alex Slobodkin/iStockphoto. (br) George F. Mobley/National Geographic Image Collection. (cl) Asia Images Group Pte Ltd/Alamy Images. (tl) Rosemarie Gearhart/iStockphoto. (tr) Csaba Vanyi/Shutterstock. 298 (bl) Nick Kennedy/Alamy Images. (br) Ryan M. Bolton/Shutterstock. (cl) Image Source Pink/Alamy Images. (cr) Creatas/Jupiterimages. (tl) PhotoAlto/Alamy Images. 299 (bl) PhotoDisc/Getty Images. (br) Anna Sedneva/Shutterstock. (cl) Tischenko Irina/Shutterstock. (cr) jamie cross/Shutterstock. (tc) PhotoDisc/Getty Images. (tl) Artville. (tr) Blend Images/Alamy Images. 300 (bl) PureStock/SuperStock. (bl) Michael and Patricia Fogden/Minden Pictures/National Geographic Image Collection. (br) PhotoDisc/Getty Images. (cl) David Madison/Digital Vision/Jupiterimages. (cr) cynoclub/Shutterstock. (tr) Polka Dot Images/Jupiterimages. 301 (bl) Corel. (br) David Chasey/Photodisc/Jupiterimages. (cl) colin streater/Alamy Images. (cr) Bettmann/Corbis. (tl) Diane N. Ennis/Shutterstock. 302 (cl) Holly Kuchera/Shutterstock. (cr) Ben Blankenburg/iStockphoto. (tl) Image Source/Alamy Images. (tr) Clint Scholz/iStockphoto. 303 (bl) Thomas M Perkins/Shutterstock. (bl) Image Source/Alamy Images. (cc) Sergey Peterman/Shutterstock. (cl) Creatas Images/Jupiterimages. (cr) Image Club. (tl) Irina Fischer/Shutterstock. (tr) BananaStock/Jupiterimages. 304 (bl) Zsolt, Biczó/Shutterstock. (br) Ulrich Niehoff/imagebroker/Alamy Images. (cl)

age fotostock/SuperStock. (cr) Thomas Perkins/iStockphoto. (tl) Robert Madden/National Geographic Image Collection. (tl) Corbis. 305 (bl) Howard Noel/iStockphoto. (cl) Michael Newman/PhotoEdit. (cr) Artville. (tc) erdem/Shutterstock. (tl) jamie cross/Shutterstock. (tr) Polka Dot Images/Jupiterimages. 306 (bl) Image Source/Jupiterimages. (br) PE Forsberg/Alamy Images. (cl) Wolf Design/Shutterstock. (tl) John Foxx Images/Imagestate. (tr) Design Pics/Jupiterimages. 307 (bl) Amanda Rohde/iStockphoto. (br) GlowImages/Alamy Images. (cl) Sven Hoppe/Shutterstock. (cr) DigitalStock/Corbis. (tl) Melville B. Grosvenor/National Geographic Image Collection. (tr) Jose Luis Pelaez Inc/Jupiterimages. 308 (bc) jamie cross/Shutterstock. (bl) Heinrich van den Berg/Getty Images. (br) erdem/Shutterstock. (cl) Digital Vision/Getty Images. (cl) Nicholas Eveleigh/Alamy Images. (tr) Photodisc/Getty Images. 309 (bl) Eric Gevaert/iStockphoto. (br) Martin Harvey/Alamy Images. (cl) Jim Arbogast/Digital Vision/Jupiterimages. (cr) Lee Prince/Shutterstock. (tl) Petar Paunchev/Alamy Images. (tr) John Giustina/Getty Images. 310 (bl) Sebastian Crocker/Shutterstock. (br) P. Broze & A. Chederros/ONOKY - Photononstop/Alamy Images. (cl) Image Box Uk Ltd/Alamy Images. (cr) Skip O'Donnell/iStockphoto. (tl) David Hardman/iStockphoto. (tr) Blend Images/Jose Luis Pelaez Inc/Getty Images. 311 (bl) James Osmond/Alamy Images. (cl) Mike Theiss/National Geographic Image Collection. (tl) jamie cross/Shutterstock. (tr) erdem/Shutterstock.

Illustrator Credits

4 Peter Grosshauser. 34 Mapping Specialists, Ltd. 72 Alessia Girasole. 97–101 Amanda Hall. 104 Don Tate. 128 Alessia Girasole. 140 Rob McClurkan; 172-173 Red Hansen; 176-189 Frank Morrison; 196 Sachiko Yoshikawa; 198 Frank Morrison. 206–208, 210 Rob McClurkan. 213, 215, 217, 219, 221 Annie Bissett. 224 Rob McClurkan. 227–231 Anne Wilson. 232 Steve Bjorkman. 233 Jannie Ho. 234 Steve Bjorkman. 235 Mapping Specialists, Ltd. 236–258, 260, 266, 268 Valeria Docampo. 270 Mapping Specialists, Ltd.

California Common Core State Standards

SE Pages	Lesson	Code	Standard
2–3	**Unit Launch:** Share What You Know		With prompting and support, read informational texts appropriately complex for grade 1.
		CA CC.1.Rinf.10.a	**Activate prior knowledge related to the information and events in a text. CA**
		CA CC.1.SL.4	Describe people, places, things, and events with relevant details, expressing ideas and feelings clearly.
		CA CC.1.SL.5	Add drawings or other visual displays to descriptions when appropriate to clarify ideas, thoughts, and feelings.
4	**Part 1:** **Language:** Compare and Contrast	CA CC.1.SL.4	Describe people, places, things, and events with relevant details, expressing ideas and feelings clearly.
		CA CC.1.SL.4.a	**Memorize and recite poems, rhymes, and songs with expression. CA**
5	**Science Vocabulary:** Key Words		With guidance and support from adults, demonstrate understanding of word relationships and nuances in word meanings.
		CA CC.1.L.5.b	Define words by category and by one or more key attributes (e.g., a *duck* is a bird that swims; a *tiger* is a large cat with stripes).
6	**Thinking Map:** Compare and Contrast		With prompting and support, read informational texts appropriately complex for grade 1.
		CA CC.1.Rinf.10.a	**Activate prior knowledge related to the information and events in a text. CA**
		CA CC.1.SL.4	Describe people, places, things, and events with relevant details, expressing ideas and feelings clearly.
7	**Academic Vocabulary:** More Key Words		Determine or clarify the meaning of unknown and multiple-meaning words and phrases based on *grade 1 reading and content,* choosing flexibly from an array of strategies.
		CA CC.1.L.4.a	Use sentence-level context as a clue to the meaning of a word or phrase.
		CA CC.1.L.6	Use words and phrases acquired through conversations, reading and being read to, and responding to texts, including using frequently occurring conjunctions to signal simple relationships (e.g., *because*).
8	**Selection 1 Preview:** Read a Story		Read with sufficient accuracy and fluency to support comprehension.
		CA CC.1.Rfou.4.a	Read on-level text with purpose and understanding.
9-28	**Selection 1: Story** For Pete's Sake	CA CC.1.Rlit.10	With prompting and support, read prose and poetry of appropriate complexity for grade 1.
29	**Meet the Author:** Writer's Craft	CA CC.1.Rlit.4	Identify words and phrases in stories or poems that suggest feelings or appeal to the senses. **(See grade 1 Language standards 4–6 for additional expectations.) CA**

California Common Core State Standards, *continued*

SE Pages	Lesson	Code	Standard
30	**Think and Respond:** Talk About It	CA CC.1.Rlit.1	Ask and answer questions about key details in a text.
		CA CC.1.Rlit.3	Describe characters, settings, and major events in a story, using key details.
		CA CC.1.Rlit.9	Compare and contrast the adventures and experiences of characters in stories.
		CA CC.1.SL.6	Produce complete sentences when appropriate to task and situation. (See grade 1 Language standards 1 and 3 for specific expectations.)
	Think and Respond: Write About It	CA CC.1.W.8	With guidance and support from adults, recall information from experiences or gather information from provided sources to answer a question.
		CA CC.1.L.6	Use words and phrases acquired through conversations, reading and being read to, and responding to texts, including using frequently occurring conjunctions to signal simple relationships (e.g., *because*).
31	**Reread and Compare:** Compare Characters	CA CC.1.Rlit.3	Describe characters, settings, and major events in a story, using key details.
		CA CC.1.Rlit.7	Use illustrations and details in a story to describe its characters, setting, or events.
		CA CC.1.W.8	With guidance and support from adults, recall information from experiences or gather information from provided sources to answer a question.
		CA CC.1.SL.1	Participate in collaborative conversations with diverse partners about *grade 1 topics and texts* with peers and adults in small and larger groups.
32	**Word Work:** Synonyms	CA CC.1.L.5	With guidance and support from adults, demonstrate understanding of word relationships and nuances in word meanings.
33–37	**Selection 2:** Science Article Alligators	CA CC.1.Rinf.10	With prompting and support, read informational texts appropriately complex for grade 1.
38	**Respond and Extend:** Compare Genres	CA CC.1.Rlit.5	Explain major differences between books that tell stories and books that give information, drawing on a wide reading of a range of text types.
		CA CC.1.Rinf.9	Identify basic similarities in and differences between two texts on the same topic (e.g., in illustrations, descriptions, or procedures).
39	**Grammar:** Complete Sentences		Demonstrate command of the conventions of standard English grammar and usage when writing or speaking.
		CA CC.1.L.1.j	Produce and expand complete simple and compound declarative, interrogative, imperative, and exclamatory sentences in response to prompts.
			Demonstrate command of the conventions of standard English capitalization, punctuation, and spelling when writing.
		CA CC.1.L.2.b	Use end punctuation for sentences.

SE Pages	Lesson	Code	Standard
40	**Part 2:** **Language:** Give Information	CA CC.1.SL.4	Describe people, places, things, and events with relevant details, expressing ideas and feelings clearly.
		CA CC.1.SL.4.a	**Memorize and recite poems, rhymes, and songs with expression. CA**
41	**Science Vocabulary:** Key Words		With guidance and support from adults, demonstrate understanding of word relationships and nuances in word meanings.
		CA CC.1.L.5.d	Distinguish shades of meaning among verbs differing in manner (e.g., *look, peek, glance, stare, glare, scowl*) and adjectives differing in intensity (e.g., *large, gigantic*) by defining or choosing them or by acting out the meanings.
42	**Thinking Map:** Categorize Details		With guidance and support from adults, demonstrate understanding of word relationships and nuances in word meanings.
		CA CC.1.L.5.a	Sort words into categories (e.g., colors, clothing) to gain a sense of the concepts the categories represent.
		CA CC.1.L.5.d	Distinguish shades of meaning among verbs differing in manner (e.g., *look, peek, glance, stare, glare, scowl*) and adjectives differing in intensity (e.g., *large, gigantic*) by defining or choosing them or by acting out the meanings.
43	**Academic Vocabulary:** More Key Words		Determine or clarify the meaning of unknown and multiple-meaning words and phrases based on *grade 1 reading and content,* choosing flexibly from an array of strategies.
		CA CC.1.L.4.a	Use sentence-level context as a clue to the meaning of a word or phrase.
44	**Selection 1 Preview:** Read a Fact Book	CA CC.1.Rinf.5	Know and use various text **structures (e.g., sequence) and text** features (e.g., headings, tables of contents, glossaries, electronic menus, icons) to locate key facts or information in a text. **CA**
			With prompting and support, read informational texts appropriately complex for grade 1.
		CA CC.1.Rinf.10.a	**Activate prior knowledge related to the information and events in a text. CA**
45–57	**Selection 1:** Fact Book Slither, Slide, Hop, and Run	CA CC.1.Rinf.10	With prompting and support, read informational texts appropriately complex for grade 1.
58	**Think and Respond:** Talk About It	CA CC.1.Rinf.1	Ask and answer questions about key details in a text.
		CA CC.1.SL.6	Produce complete sentences when appropriate to task and situation. (See grade 1 Language standards 1 and 3 for specific expectations.)
	Think and Respond: Write About It	CA CC.1.W.8	With guidance and support from adults, recall information from experiences or gather information from provided sources to answer a question.
		CA CC.1.L.6	Use words and phrases acquired through conversations, reading and being read to, and responding to texts, including using frequently occurring conjunctions to signal simple relationships (e.g., *because*).

California Common Core State Standards, continued

SE Pages	Lesson	Code	Standard
59	**Reread and Summarize:** Categorize Details	CA CC.1.Rinf.2	Identify the main topic and retell key details of a text.
		CA CC.1.W.8	With guidance and support from adults, recall information from experiences or gather information from provided sources to answer a question.
		CA CC.1.SL.4	Describe people, places, things, and events with relevant details, expressing ideas and feelings clearly.
			With guidance and support from adults, demonstrate understanding of word relationships and nuances in word meanings.
		CA CC.1.L.5.a	Sort words into categories (e.g., colors, clothing) to gain a sense of the concepts the categories represent.
		CA CC.1.L.5.b	Define words by category and by one or more key attributes (e.g., a *duck* is a bird that swims; a *tiger* is a large cat with stripes).
		CA CC.1.L.6	Use words and phrases acquired through conversations, reading and being read to, and responding to texts, including using frequently occurring conjunctions to signal simple relationships (e.g., *because*).
60	**Word Work:** Antonyms	CA CC.1.L.5	With guidance and support from adults, demonstrate understanding of word relationships and nuances in word meanings.
61–63	**Selection 2:** Photo Journal My Crittercam Journal	CA CC.1.Rinf.10	With prompting and support, read informational texts appropriately complex for grade 1.
		CA CC.1.Rinf.10.a	**Activate prior knowledge related to the information and events in a text. CA**
64	**Respond and Extend:** Compare Genres	CA CC.1.Rinf.9	Identify basic similarities in and differences between two texts on the same topic (e.g., in illustrations, descriptions, or procedures).
		CA CC.1.SL.1	Participate in collaborative conversations with diverse partners about *grade 1 topics and texts* with peers and adults in small and larger groups.
		CA CC.1.SL.4	Describe people, places, things, and events with relevant details, expressing ideas and feelings clearly.
		CA CC.1.L.6	Use words and phrases acquired through conversations, reading and being read to, and responding to texts, including using frequently occurring conjunctions to signal simple relationships (e.g., *because*).
65	**Grammar and Spelling:** Subject-Verb Agreement		Demonstrate command of the conventions of standard English grammar and usage when writing or speaking.
		CA CC.1.L.1.c	Use singular and plural nouns with matching verbs in basic sentences (e.g., *He hops; We hop*).

SE Pages	Lesson	Code	Standard
66–67	**Writing Project:** Write Like a Scientist	CA CC.1.W.2	Write informative/explanatory texts in which they name a topic, supply some facts about the topic, and provide some sense of closure.
		CA CC.1.W.5	With guidance and support from adults, focus on a topic, respond to questions and suggestions from peers, and add details to strengthen writing as needed.
		CA CC.1.W.8	With guidance and support from adults, recall information from experiences or gather information from provided sources to answer a question.
		CA CC.1.SL.1.a	Participate in collaborative conversations with diverse partners about *grade 1 topics and texts* with peers and adults in small and larger groups. Follow agreed-upon rules for discussions (e.g., listening to others with care, speaking one at a time about the topics and texts under discussion).
		CA CC.1.SL.4	Describe people, places, things, and events with relevant details, expressing ideas and feelings clearly.
		CA CC.1.SL.5	Add drawings or other visual displays to descriptions when appropriate to clarify ideas, thoughts, and feelings.
		CA CC.1.L.1.j	Demonstrate command of the conventions of standard English grammar and usage when writing or speaking. Produce and expand complete simple and compound declarative, interrogative, imperative, and exclamatory sentences in response to prompts.
		CA CC.1.L.2.b	Demonstrate command of the conventions of standard English capitalization, punctuation, and spelling when writing. Use end punctuation for sentences.
		CA CC.1.L.2.d	Use conventional spelling for words with common spelling patterns and for frequently occurring irregular words.
		CA CC.1.L.2.e	Spell untaught words phonetically, drawing on phonemic awareness and spelling conventions.
		CA CC.1.L.6	Use words and phrases acquired through conversations, reading and being read to, and responding to texts, including using frequently occurring conjunctions to signal simple relationships (e.g., *because*).

California Common Core State Standards, *continued*

SE Pages	Lesson	Code	Standard
68–69	**Unit Wrap-Up:** Share Your Ideas	CA CC.1.W.8	With guidance and support from adults, recall information from experiences or gather information from provided sources to answer a question.
		CA CC.1.SL.1	Participate in collaborative conversations with diverse partners about *grade 1 topics and texts* with peers and adults in small and larger groups.
		CA CC.1.SL.1.a	Follow agreed-upon rules for discussions (e.g., listening to others with care, speaking one at a time about the topics and texts under discussion).
		CA CC.1.SL.1.b	Build on others' talk in conversations by responding to the comments of others through multiple exchanges.
		CA CC.1.SL.1.c	Ask questions to clear up any confusion about the topics and texts under discussion.
		CA CC.1.SL.3	Ask and answer questions about what a speaker says in order to gather additional information or clarify something that is not understood.
		CA CC.1.SL.4	Describe people, places, things, and events with relevant details, expressing ideas and feelings clearly.
		CA CC.1.SL.5	Add drawings or other visual displays to descriptions when appropriate to clarify ideas, thoughts, and feelings.
		CA CC.1.L.6	Use words and phrases acquired through conversations, reading and being read to, and responding to texts, including using frequently occurring conjunctions to signal simple relationships (e.g., *because*).

California Common Core State Standards

SE Pages	Lesson	Code	Standard
70–71	**Unit Launch:** Share What You Know		With prompting and support, read informational texts appropriately complex for grade 1.
		CA CC.1.Rinf.10.a	**Activate prior knowledge related to the information and events in a text. CA**
		CA CC.1.SL.4	Describe people, places, things, and events with relevant details, expressing ideas and feelings clearly.
		CA CC.1.SL.5	Add drawings or other visual displays to descriptions when appropriate to clarify ideas, thoughts, and feelings.
72	**Part 1:** **Language:** Explain	CA CC.1.SL.4	Describe people, places, things, and events with relevant details, expressing ideas and feelings clearly.
		CA CC.1.SL.4.a	**Memorize and recite poems, rhymes, and songs with expression. CA**
73	**Science Vocabulary:** Key Words	CA CC.1.SL.4	Describe people, places, things, and events with relevant details, expressing ideas and feelings clearly.
			Determine or clarify the meaning of unknown and multiple-meaning words and phrases based on *grade 1 reading and content,* choosing flexibly from an array of strategies.
		CA CC.1.L.4.a	Use sentence-level context as a clue to the meaning of a word or phrase.
74	**Thinking Map:** ind Cause and Effect	CA CC.1.Rinf.5	Know and use various text **structures (e.g., sequence) and text** features (e.g., headings, tables of contents, glossaries, electronic menus, icons) to locate key facts or information in a text. **CA**
			With prompting and support, read informational texts appropriately complex for grade 1.
		CA CC.1.Rinf.10.a	**Activate prior knowledge related to the information and events in a text. CA**
		CA CC.1.SL.4	Describe people, places, things, and events with relevant details, expressing ideas and feelings clearly.
75	**Academic Vocabulary:** More Key Words		Know and apply grade-level phonics and word analysis skills in decoding words **both in isolation and in text. CA**
		CA CC.1.Rfou.3.d	Use knowledge that every syllable must have a vowel sound to determine the number of syllables in a printed word.
			Determine or clarify the meaning of unknown and multiple-meaning words and phrases based on *grade 1 reading and content,* choosing flexibly from an array of strategies.
		CA CC.1.L.4.a	Use sentence-level context as a clue to the meaning of a word or phrase.
76	**Selection 1 Preview:** Read Science Nonfiction	CA CC.1.Rinf.7	Use the illustrations and details in a text to describe its key ideas.
			Read with sufficient accuracy and fluency to support comprehension.
		CA CC.1.Rfou.4.a	Read on-level text with purpose and understanding.

California Common Core State Standards, continued

SE Pages	Lesson	Code	Standard
77–93	**Selection 1:** Science Nonfiction I Face the Wind	CA CC.1.Rinf.10	With prompting and support, read informational texts appropriately complex for grade 1.
94	**Think and Respond:** Talk About It	CA CC.1.Rinf.1	Ask and answer questions about key details in a text.
		CA CC.1.Rinf.2	Identify the main topic and retell key details of a text.
		CA CC.1.Rinf.3	Describe the connection between two individuals, events, ideas, or pieces of information in a text.
		CA CC.1.SL.6	Produce complete sentences when appropriate to task and situation. (See grade 1 Language standards 1 and 3 for specific expectations.)
		CA CC.1.L.6	Use words and phrases acquired through conversations, reading and being read to, and responding to texts, including using frequently occurring conjunctions to signal simple relationships (e.g., *because*).
	Think and Respond: Write About It	CA CC.1.W.8	With guidance and support from adults, recall information from experiences or gather information from provided sources to answer a question.
		CA CC.1.Rinf.7	Use the illustrations and details in a text to describe its key ideas.
95	**Reread and Explain:** Find Cause and Effect	CA CC.1.Rinf.3	Describe the connection between two individuals, events, ideas, or pieces of information in a text.
		CA CC.1.W.8	With guidance and support from adults, recall information from experiences or gather information from provided sources to answer a question.
96	**Word Work:** Compound Words	CA CC.1.L.4	Determine or clarify the meaning of unknown and multiple-meaning words and phrases based on *grade 1 reading and content,* choosing flexibly from an array of strategies.
97–101	**Selection 2:** Legend Wind Eagle: A Native American legend	CA CC.1.Rlit.10	With prompting and support, read prose and poetry of appropriate complexity for grade 1.
102	**Respond and Extend:** Character's Action	CA CC.1.Rlit.3	Describe characters, settings, and major events in a story, using key details.
		CA CC.1.SL.1	Participate in collaborative conversations with diverse partners about *grade 1 topics and texts* with peers and adults in small and larger groups.
		CA CC.1.SL.4	Describe people, places, things, and events with relevant details, expressing ideas and feelings clearly.

SE Pages	Lesson	Code	Standard
103	**Grammar:** Sentence Types	CA CC.1.Rfou.1	Demonstrate understanding of the organization and basic features of print.
		CA CC.1.Rfou.1.a	Recognize the distinguishing features of a sentence (e.g., first word, capitalization, ending punctuation).
			Demonstrate command of the conventions of standard English grammar and usage when writing or speaking.
		CA CC.1.L.1.j	Produce and expand complete simple and compound declarative, interrogative, imperative, and exclamatory sentences in response to prompts.
			Demonstrate command of the conventions of standard English capitalization, punctuation, and spelling when writing.
		CA CC.1.L.2.b	Use end punctuation for sentences.
104	**Part 2:Language:** Express Ideas	CA CC.1.SL.4	Describe people, places, things, and events with relevant details, expressing ideas and feelings clearly.
		CA CC.1.SL.4.a	**Memorize and recite poems, rhymes, and songs with expression. CA**
105	**Science Vocabulary:** Key Words	CA CC.1.SL.1	Participate in collaborative conversations with diverse partners about *grade 1 topics and texts* with peers and adults in small and larger groups.
			Determine or clarify the meaning of unknown and multiple-meaning words and phrases based on *grade 1 reading and content,* choosing flexibly from an array of strategies.
		CA CC.1.L.4.a	Use sentence-level context as a clue to the meaning of a word or phrase.
106	**Thinking Map:** Classify Details	CA CC.1.W.8	With guidance and support from adults, recall information from experiences or gather information from provided sources to answer a question.
		CA CC.1.SL.4	Describe people, places, things, and events with relevant details, expressing ideas and feelings clearly.
			With guidance and support from adults, demonstrate understanding of word relationships and nuances in word meanings.
		CA CC.1.L.5.a	Sort words into categories (e.g., colors, clothing) to gain a sense of the concepts the categories represent.
107	**Academic Vocabulary:** More Key Words		Determine or clarify the meaning of unknown and multiple-meaning words and phrases based on *grade 1 reading and content,* choosing flexibly from an array of strategies.
		CA CC.1.L.4.a	Use sentence-level context as a clue to the meaning of a word or phrase.
108	**Selection 1 Preview:** Read Realistic Fiction		Read with sufficient accuracy and fluency to support comprehension.
		CA CC.1.Rfou.4.a	Read on-level text with purpose and understanding.
109–124	**Selection 1:** Realistic Fiction A Year for Kiko	CA CC.1.Rlit.10	With prompting and support, read prose and poetry of appropriate complexity for grade 1.

California Common Core State Standards, *continued*

SE Pages	Lesson	Code	Standard
125	**Meet the Author:** Writer's Craft	CA CC.1.L.5	With guidance and support from adults, demonstrate understanding of word relationships and nuances in word meanings.
126	**Think and Respond:** Talk About It	CA CC.1.Rlit.1	Ask and answer questions about key details in a text.
		CA CC.1.Rlit.3	Describe characters, settings, and major events in a story, using key details.
		CA CC.1.SL.4	Describe people, places, things, and events with relevant details, expressing ideas and feelings clearly.
		CA CC.1.SL.6	Produce complete sentences when appropriate to task and situation. (See grade 1 Language standards 1 and 3 for specific expectations.)
		CA CC.1.L.6	Use words and phrases acquired through conversations, reading and being read to, and responding to texts, including using frequently occurring conjunctions to signal simple relationships (e.g., *because*).
	Think and Respond: Write About It	CA CC.1.W.8	With guidance and support from adults, recall information from experiences or gather information from provided sources to answer a question.
		CA CC.1.Rlit.4	Identify words and phrases in stories or poems that suggest feelings or appeal to the senses. **(See grade 1 Language standards 4–6 for additional expectations.) CA**
127	**Reread and Retell:** Classify Details	CA CC.1.Rlit.3	Describe characters, settings, and major events in a story, using key details.
		CA CC.1.Rlit.7	Use illustrations and details in a story to describe its characters, setting, or events.
		CA CC.1.SL.1	Determine or clarify the meaning of unknown and multiple-meaning words and phrases based on *grade 1 reading and content,* choosing flexibly from an array of strategies.
		CA CC.1.L.5.a	Sort words into categories (e.g., colors, clothing) to gain a sense of the concepts the categories represent.
128	**Word Work:** Compound Words	CA CC.1.L.4	Determine or clarify the meaning of unknown and multiple-meaning words and phrases based on *grade 1 reading and content,* choosing flexibly from an array of strategies.
129–131	**Selection 2:** Interview Chasing Storms with Tim Samaras	CA CC.1.Rinf.10	With prompting and support, read informational texts appropriately complex for grade 1.

SE Pages	Lesson	Code	Standard
132	**Respond and Extend:** Compare Genres	CA CC.1.Rlit.5	Explain major differences between books that tell stories and books that give information, drawing on a wide reading of a range of text types.
		CA CC.1.Rinf.9	Identify basic similarities in and differences between two texts on the same topic (e.g., in illustrations, descriptions, or procedures).
		CA CC.1.SL.1	Participate in collaborative conversations with diverse partners about *grade 1 topics and texts* with peers and adults in small and larger groups.
		CA CC.1.SL.4	Describe people, places, things, and events with relevant details, expressing ideas and feelings clearly.
		CA CC.1.L.6	Use words and phrases acquired through conversations, reading and being read to, and responding to texts, including using frequently occurring conjunctions to signal simple relationships (e.g., *because*).
133	**Grammar:** Ask Questions		Demonstrate command of the conventions of standard English grammar and usage when writing or speaking.
		CA CC.1.L.1.j	Produce and expand complete simple and compound declarative, interrogative, imperative, and exclamatory sentences in response to prompts.

California Common Core State Standards, *continued*

SE Pages	Lesson	Code	Standard
134–135	**Writing Project:** Write Like a Reporter	CA CC.1.W.2	Write informative/explanatory texts in which they name a topic, supply some facts about the topic, and provide some sense of closure.
		CA CC.1.W.5	With guidance and support from adults, focus on a topic, respond to questions and suggestions from peers, and add details to strengthen writing as needed.
		CA CC.1.W.8	With guidance and support from adults, recall information from experiences or gather information from provided sources to answer a question.
			Participate in collaborative conversations with diverse partners about *grade 1 topics and texts* with peers and adults in small and larger groups.
		CA CC.1.SL.1.a	Follow agreed-upon rules for discussions (e.g., listening to others with care, speaking one at a time about the topics and texts under discussion).
		CA CC.1.SL.4	Describe people, places, things, and events with relevant details, expressing ideas and feelings clearly.
			Demonstrate command of the conventions of standard English grammar and usage when writing or speaking.
		CA CC.1.L.1.j	Produce and expand complete simple and compound declarative, interrogative, imperative, and exclamatory sentences in response to prompts.
			Demonstrate command of the conventions of standard English capitalization, punctuation, and spelling when writing.
		CA CC.1.L.2.b	Use end punctuation for sentences.
		CA CC.1.L.2.d	Use conventional spelling for words with common spelling patterns and for frequently occurring irregular words.
		CA CC.1.L.2.e	Spell untaught words phonetically, drawing on phonemic awareness and spelling conventions.
		CA CC.1.L.6	Use words and phrases acquired through conversations, reading and being read to, and responding to texts, including using frequently occurring conjunctions to signal simple relationships (e.g., *because*).
130–131	**Unit Wrap-Up:** Share Your Ideas	CA CC.1.W.8	With guidance and support from adults, recall information from experiences or gather information from provided sources to answer a question.
		CA CC.1.SL.1	Participate in collaborative conversations with diverse partners about *grade 1 topics and texts* with peers and adults in small and larger groups.
		CA CC.1.SL.4	Describe people, places, things, and events with relevant details, expressing ideas and feelings clearly.
		CA CC.1.SL.5	Add drawings or other visual displays to descriptions when appropriate to clarify ideas, thoughts, and feelings.
		CA CC.1.L.6	Use words and phrases acquired through conversations, reading and being read to, and responding to texts, including using frequently occurring conjunctions to signal simple relationships (e.g., *because*).

California Common Core State Standards

SE Pages	Lesson	Code	Standard
138–139	**Unit Launch:** Share What You Know		With prompting and support, read prose and poetry of appropriate complexity for grade 1.
		CA CC.1.Rlit.10.a	**Activate prior knowledge related to the information and events in a text. CA**
		CA CC.1.SL.1	Participate in collaborative conversations with diverse partners about *grade 1 topics and texts* with peers and adults in small and larger groups.
140	**Part 1:** **Language:** Express Opinions	CA CC.1.SL.4	Describe people, places, things, and events with relevant details, expressing ideas and feelings clearly.
		CA CC.1.SL.4.a	**Memorize and recite poems, rhymes, and songs with expression. CA**
141	**Social Studies Vocabulary:** Key Words	CA CC.1.SL.1	Participate in collaborative conversations with diverse partners about *grade 1 topics and texts* with peers and adults in small and larger groups.
		CA CC.1.SL.4	Describe people, places, things, and events with relevant details, expressing ideas and feelings clearly.
			Determine or clarify the meaning of unknown and multiple-meaning words and phrases based on *grade 1 reading and content,* choosing flexibly from an array of strategies.
		CA CC.1.L.4.a	Use sentence-level context as a clue to the meaning of a word or phrase.
142	**Thinking Map:** Identify Main Idea and Details	CA CC.1.Rinf.5	Know and use various text **structures (e.g., sequence) and text** features (e.g., headings, tables of contents, glossaries, electronic menus, icons) to locate key facts or information in a text. **CA**
		CA CC.1.SL.1	Participate in collaborative conversations with diverse partners about *grade 1 topics and texts* with peers and adults in small and larger groups.
		CA CC.1.SL.1.a	Follow agreed-upon rules for discussions (e.g., listening to others with care, speaking one at a time about the topics and texts under discussion).
		CA CC.1.SL.1.b	Build on others' talk in conversations by responding to the comments of others through multiple exchanges.
		CA CC.1.SL.1.c	Ask questions to clear up any confusion about the topics and texts under discussion.
143	**Academic Vocabulary:** More Key Words		Determine or clarify the meaning of unknown and multiple-meaning words and phrases based on *grade 1 reading and content,* choosing flexibly from an array of strategies.
		CA CC.1.L.4.a	Use sentence-level context as a clue to the meaning of a word or phrase.
		CA CC.1.L.6	Use words and phrases acquired through conversations, reading and being read to, and responding to texts, including using frequently occurring conjunctions to signal simple relationships (e.g., *because*).

California Common Core State Standards, *continued*

SE Pages	Lesson	Code	Standard
144	**Selection 1 Preview:** Read a History Article	CA CC.1.Rinf.5	Know and use various text **structures (e.g., sequence) and text** features (e.g., headings, tables of contents, glossaries, electronic menus, icons) to locate key facts or information in a text. **CA**
			Read with sufficient accuracy and fluency to support comprehension.
		CA CC.1.Rfou.4.a	Read on-level text with purpose and understanding.
145–161	**Selection 1: History Article** Communication Then and Now	CA CC.1.Rinf.10	With prompting and support, read informational texts appropriately complex for grade 1.
162	**Think and Respond:** Talk About It	CA CC.1.Rinf.1	Ask and answer questions about key details in a text.
		CA CC.1.Rinf.2	Identify the main topic and retell key details of a text.
		CA CC.1.Rinf.7	Use the illustrations and details in a text to describe its key ideas.
		CA CC.1.SL.6	Produce complete sentences when appropriate to task and situation. (See grade 1 Language standards 1 and 3 for specific expectations.)
		CA CC.1.L.6	Use words and phrases acquired through conversations, reading and being read to, and responding to texts, including using frequently occurring conjunctions to signal simple relationships (e.g., *because*).
	Think and Respond: Write About It	CA CC.1.W.8	With guidance and support from adults, recall information from experiences or gather information from provided sources to answer a question.
		CA CC.1.L.6	Use words and phrases acquired through conversations, reading and being read to, and responding to texts, including using frequently occurring conjunctions to signal simple relationships (e.g., *because*).
163	**Reread and Summarize:** Identify Main Idea and Details	CA CC.1.Rinf.1	Ask and answer questions about key details in a text.
		CA CC.1.Rinf.7	Use the illustrations and details in a text to describe its key ideas.
		CA CC.1.W.8	With guidance and support from adults, recall information from experiences or gather information from provided sources to answer a question.
		CA CC.1.SL.1	Participate in collaborative conversations with diverse partners about *grade 1 topics and texts* with peers and adults in small and larger groups.
			With guidance and support from adults, demonstrate understanding of word relationships and nuances in word meanings.
		CA CC.1.L.5.a	Sort words into categories (e.g., colors, clothing) to gain a sense of the concepts the categories represent.

SE Pages	Lesson	Code	Standard
164	**Word Work:** Alphabetize and Use a Dictionary	CA CC.1.Rfou.1	Demonstrate understanding of the organization and basic features of print.
165–169	**Selection 2:** Blog My Space Adventures	CA CC.1.Rinf.10	With prompting and support, read informational texts appropriately complex for grade 1.
170	**Respond and Extend:** Compare Genres	CA CC.1.Rinf.9	Identify basic similarities in and differences between two texts on the same topic (e.g., in illustrations, descriptions, or procedures).
		CA CC.1.SL.1	Participate in collaborative conversations with diverse partners about *grade 1 topics and texts* with peers and adults in small and larger groups.
		CA CC.1.L.6	Use words and phrases acquired through conversations, reading and being read to, and responding to texts, including using frequently occurring conjunctions to signal simple relationships (e.g., *because*).
171	**Grammar and Spelling:** Past Tense Verbs		Know and apply grade-level phonics and word analysis skills in decoding words **both in isolation and in text. CA**
		CA CC.1.Rfou.3.f	Read words with inflectional endings.
			Demonstrate command of the conventions of standard English grammar and usage when writing or speaking.
		CA CC.1.L.1.e	Use verbs to convey a sense of past, present, and future (e.g., *Yesterday I walked home; Today I walk home; Tomorrow I will walk home*).
			Determine or clarify the meaning of unknown and multiple-meaning words and phrases based on *grade 1 reading and content,* choosing flexibly from an array of strategies.
		CA CC.1.L.4.c	Identify frequently occurring root words (e.g., *look*) and their inflectional forms (e.g., *looks, looked, looking*).
172	**Part 2: Language:** Express Feelings		Describe people, places, things, and events with relevant details, expressing ideas and feelings clearly.
		CA CC.1.SL.4.a	**Memorize and recite poems, rhymes, and songs with expression. CA**
173	**Social Studies Vocabulary:** Key Words		Determine or clarify the meaning of unknown and multiple-meaning words and phrases based on *grade 1 reading and content,* choosing flexibly from an array of strategies.
		CA CC.1.L.4.a	Use sentence-level context as a clue to the meaning of a word or phrase.
			With guidance and support from adults, demonstrate understanding of word relationships and nuances in word meanings.
		CA CC.1.L.5.a	Sort words into categories (e.g., colors, clothing) to gain a sense of the concepts the categories represent.
174	**Thinking Map:** Describe Characters' Feelings	CA CC.1.Rlit.3	Describe characters, settings, and major events in a story, using key details.
		CA CC.1.SL.4	Describe people, places, things, and events with relevant details, expressing ideas and feelings clearly.

California Common Core State Standards, *continued*

SE Pages	Lesson	Code	Standard
175	**Academic Vocabulary:** More Key Words		Determine or clarify the meaning of unknown and multiple-meaning words and phrases based on *grade 1 reading and content,* choosing flexibly from an array of strategies.
		CA CC.1.L.4.a	Use sentence-level context as a clue to the meaning of a word or phrase.
176	**Selection 1 Preview:** Read a Story		Read with sufficient accuracy and fluency to support comprehension.
		CA CC.1.Rfou.4.a	Read on-level text with purpose and understanding.
177–188	**Selection 1:** Realistic Fiction A New Old Tune	CA CC.1.Rlit.10	With prompting and support, read prose and poetry of appropriate complexity for grade 1.
189	**Meet the Author:** Writer's Craft	CA CC.1.Rlit.7	Use illustrations and details in a story to describe its characters, setting, or events.
190	**Think and Respond:** Talk About It	CA CC.1.Rlit.1	Ask and answer questions about key details in a text.
		CA CC.1.Rlit.2	Retell stories, including key details, and demonstrate understanding of their central message or lesson.
		CA CC.1.SL.6	Produce complete sentences when appropriate to task and situation. (See grade 1 Language standards 1 and 3 for specific expectations.)
	Think and Respond: Write About It	CA CC.1.W.8	With guidance and support from adults, recall information from experiences or gather information from provided sources to answer a question.
		CA CC.1.L.6	Use words and phrases acquired through conversations, reading and being read to, and responding to texts, including using frequently occurring conjunctions to signal simple relationships (e.g., *because*).
191	**Reread and Retell:** Describe Characters' Feelings	CA CC.1.Rlit.3	Describe characters, settings, and major events in a story, using key details.
		CA CC.1.Rlit.7	Use illustrations and details in a story to describe its characters, setting, or events.
192	**Word Work:** Alphabetize and Use a Dictionary	CA CC.1.Rfou.1	Demonstrate understanding of the organization and basic features of print.
193–197	**Selection 2:** Poem Invention Poems	CA CC.1.Rlit.10	With prompting and support, read prose and poetry of appropriate complexity for grade 1.
198	**Respond and Extend:** Compare Genres	CA CC.1.SL.1	Participate in collaborative conversations with diverse partners about *grade 1 topics and texts* with peers and adults in small and larger groups.
		CA CC.1.SL.4	Describe people, places, things, and events with relevant details, expressing ideas and feelings clearly.
		CA CC.1.L.6	Use words and phrases acquired through conversations, reading and being read to, and responding to texts, including using frequently occurring conjunctions to signal simple relationships (e.g., *because*).

SE Pages	Lesson	Code	Standard
199	**Grammar:** Future Tense Verbs		Demonstrate command of the conventions of standard English grammar and usage when writing or speaking.
		CA CC.1.L.1.e	Use verbs to convey a sense of past, present, and future (e.g., *Yesterday I walked home; Today I walk home; Tomorrow I will walk home*).
200–201	**Writing Project:** Write as a Friend	CA CC.1.W.2	Write informative/explanatory texts in which they name a topic, supply some facts about the topic, and provide some sense of closure.
		CA CC.1.W.5	With guidance and support from adults, focus on a topic, respond to questions and suggestions from peers, and add details to strengthen writing as needed.
		CA CC.1.W.8	With guidance and support from adults, recall information from experiences or gather information from provided sources to answer a question.
		CA CC.1.SL.4	Describe people, places, things, and events with relevant details, expressing ideas and feelings clearly.
			Demonstrate command of the conventions of standard English grammar and usage when writing or speaking.
		CA CC.1.L.1.e	Use verbs to convey a sense of past, present, and future (e.g., *Yesterday I walked home; Today I walk home; Tomorrow I will walk home*).
			Demonstrate command of the conventions of standard English capitalization, punctuation, and spelling when writing.
		CA CC.1.L.2.d	Use conventional spelling for words with common spelling patterns and for frequently occurring irregular words.
		CA CC.1.L.2.e	Spell untaught words phonetically, drawing on phonemic awareness and spelling conventions.
		CA CC.1.L.5	With guidance and support from adults, demonstrate understanding of word relationships and nuances in word meanings.

California Common Core State Standards, *continued*

SE Pages	Lesson	Code	Standard
202–203	**Unit Wrap-Up:** Share Your Ideas	CA CC.1.SL.1	Participate in collaborative conversations with diverse partners about *grade 1 topics and texts* with peers and adults in small and larger groups.
		CA CC.1.SL.1.a	Follow agreed-upon rules for discussions (e.g., listening to others with care, speaking one at a time about the topics and texts under discussion).
		CA CC.1.SL.1.b	Build on others' talk in conversations by responding to the comments of others through multiple exchanges.
		CA CC.1.SL.1.c	Ask questions to clear up any confusion about the topics and texts under discussion.
		CA CC.1.SL.4	Describe people, places, things, and events with relevant details, expressing ideas and feelings clearly.
		CA CC.1.SL.2	Ask and answer questions about key details in a text read aloud or information presented orally or through other media.
		CA CC.1.SL.2.a	**Give, restate, and follow simple two-step directions. CA**
		CA CC.1.L.5.b	Define words by category and by one or more key attributes (e.g., a *duck* is a bird that swims; a *tiger* is a large cat with stripes).
		CA CC.1.L.6	Use words and phrases acquired through conversations, reading and being read to, and responding to texts, including using frequently occurring conjunctions to signal simple relationships (e.g., *because*).

California Common Core State Standards

SE Pages	Lesson	Code	Standard
204–205	**Unit Launch:** Share What You Know		With prompting and support, read informational texts appropriately complex for grade 1.
		CA CC.1.Rinf.10.a	**Activate prior knowledge related to the information and events in a text. CA**
		CA CC.1.SL.2	Ask and answer questions about key details in a text read aloud or information presented orally or through other media.
		CA CC.1.SL.2.a	**Give, restate, and follow simple two-step directions. CA**
		CA CC.1.SL.5	Add drawings or other visual displays to descriptions when appropriate to clarify ideas, thoughts, and feelings.
206	**Part 1: Language:** Follow Directions		Ask and answer questions about key details in a text read aloud or information presented orally or through other media.
		CA CC.1.SL.2.a	**Give, restate, and follow simple two-step directions. CA**
		CA CC.1.SL.4	Describe people, places, things, and events with relevant details, expressing ideas and feelings clearly.
		CA CC.1.SL.4.a	**Memorize and recite poems, rhymes, and songs with expression. CA**
207	**Social Studies Vocabulary:** Key Words		Ask and answer questions about key details in a text read aloud or information presented orally or through other media.
		CA CC.1.SL.2.a	**Give, restate, and follow simple two-step directions. CA**
		CA CC.1.SL.4	Describe people, places, things, and events with relevant details, expressing ideas and feelings clearly.
			Determine or clarify the meaning of unknown and multiple-meaning words and phrases based on *grade 1 reading and content,* choosing flexibly from an array of strategies.
		CA CC.1.L.4.a	Use sentence-level context as a clue to the meaning of a word or phrase.
208	**Thinking Map:** Use Information	CA CC.1.SL.4	Describe people, places, things, and events with relevant details, expressing ideas and feelings clearly.
		CA CC.1.L.6	Use words and phrases acquired through conversations, reading and being read to, and responding to texts, including using frequently occurring conjunctions to signal simple relationships (e.g., *because*).
209	**Academic Vocabulary:** More Key Words		Determine or clarify the meaning of unknown and multiple-meaning words and phrases based on *grade 1 reading and content,* choosing flexibly from an array of strategies.
		CA CC.1.L.4.a	Use sentence-level context as a clue to the meaning of a word or phrase.
		CA CC.1.L.6	Use words and phrases acquired through conversations, reading and being read to, and responding to texts, including using frequently occurring conjunctions to signal simple relationships (e.g., *because*).

California Common Core State Standards, *continued*

SE Pages	Lesson	Code	Standard
210	**Selection 1 Preview:** Read Informational Text	CA CC.1.Rinf.5	Know and use various text **structures (e.g., sequence) and text** features (e.g., headings, tables of contents, glossaries, electronic menus, icons) to locate key facts or information in a text. **CA**
			Read with sufficient accuracy and fluency to support comprehension.
		CA CC.1.Rfou.4.a	Read on-level text with purpose and understanding.
211–223	**Selection 1:** Informational Text If Maps Could Talk	CA CC.1.Rinf.10	With prompting and support, read informational texts appropriately complex for grade 1.
224	**Think and Respond:** Talk About It	CA CC.1.Rinf.1	Ask and answer questions about key details in a text.
		CA CC.1.Rinf.3	Describe the connection between two individuals, events, ideas, or pieces of information in a text.
		CA CC.1.Rinf.5	Know and use various text **structures (e.g., sequence) and text** features (e.g., headings, tables of contents, glossaries, electronic menus, icons) to locate key facts or information in a text. **CA**
		CA CC.1.Rinf.8	Identify the reasons an author gives to support points in a text.
		CA CC.1.SL.6	Produce complete sentences when appropriate to task and situation. (See grade 1 Language standards 1 and 3 for specific expectations.)
		CA CC.1.L.6	Use words and phrases acquired through conversations, reading and being read to, and responding to texts, including using frequently occurring conjunctions to signal simple relationships (e.g., *because*).
	Think and Respond: Write About It	CA CC.1.Rinf.7	Use the illustrations and details in a text to describe its key ideas.
		CA CC.1.W.8	With guidance and support from adults, recall information from experiences or gather information from provided sources to answer a question.
225	**Reread and Retell:** Use Information	CA CC.1.Rinf.5	Know and use various text **structures (e.g., sequence) and text** features (e.g., headings, tables of contents, glossaries, electronic menus, icons) to locate key facts or information in a text. **CA**
		CA CC.1.SL.4	Describe people, places, things, and events with relevant details, expressing ideas and feelings clearly.
226	**Word Work:** Suffixes		Determine or clarify the meaning of unknown and multiple-meaning words and phrases based on *grade 1 reading and content,* choosing flexibly from an array of strategies.
		CA CC.1.L.4.b	Use frequently occurring affixes as a clue to the meaning of a word.
227–229	**Selection 2: Poem** Haiku	CA CC.1.Rlit.10	With prompting and support, read prose and poetry of appropriate complexity for grade 1.

SE Pages	Lesson	Code	Standard
230	**Respond and Extend:** Compare Genres	CA CC.1.Rlit.5	Explain major differences between books that tell stories and books that give information, drawing on a wide reading of a range of text types.
		CA CC.1.Rinf.9	Identify basic similarities in and differences between two texts on the same topic (e.g., in illustrations, descriptions, or procedures).
		CA CC.1.SL.4	Describe people, places, things, and events with relevant details, expressing ideas and feelings clearly.
231	**Grammar and Spelling:** Adverbs	CA CC.1.L.1	Demonstrate command of the conventions of standard English grammar and usage when writing or speaking.
			Determine or clarify the meaning of unknown and multiple-meaning words and phrases based on *grade 1 reading and content,* choosing flexibly from an array of strategies.
		CA CC.1.L.4.b	Use frequently occurring affixes as a clue to the meaning of a word.
232	**Part 2:** **Language:** Tell a Story	CA CC.1.SL.4	Describe people, places, things, and events with relevant details, expressing ideas and feelings clearly.
		CA CC.1.SL.4.a	**Memorize and recite poems, rhymes, and songs with expression. CA**
233	**Social Studies:** Key Words	CA CC.1.L.6	Use words and phrases acquired through conversations, reading and being read to, and responding to texts, including using frequently occurring conjunctions to signal simple relationships (e.g., *because*).
234	**Thinking Map:** Identify Problem and Solution	CA CC.1.Rlit.2	Retell stories, including key details, and demonstrate understanding of their central message or lesson.
		CA CC.1.SL.1	Participate in collaborative conversations with diverse partners about *grade 1 topics and texts* with peers and adults in small and larger groups.
235	**Academic Vocabulary:** More Key Words		Participate in collaborative conversations with diverse partners about *grade 1 topics and texts* with peers and adults in small and larger groups.
		CA CC.1.SL.1.c	Ask questions to clear up any confusion about the topics and texts under discussion.
			Determine or clarify the meaning of unknown and multiple-meaning words and phrases based on *grade 1 reading and content,* choosing flexibly from an array of strategies.
		CA CC.1.L.4.a	Use sentence-level context as a clue to the meaning of a word or phrase.
236	**Selection 1 Preview:** Read a Modern Fairy Tale	CA CC.1.Rlit.10	With prompting and support, read prose and poetry of appropriate complexity for grade 1.
			Read with sufficient accuracy and fluency to support comprehension.
		CA CC.1.Rfou.4.a	Read on-level text with purpose and understanding.
237–256	**Selection 1:** Modern Fairy Tale Caperucita Roja	CA CC.1.Rlit.10	With prompting and support, read prose and poetry of appropriate complexity for grade 1.

California Common Core State Standards, continued

SE Pages	Lesson	Code	Standard
257	**Meet the Author:** Writer's Craft	CA CC.1.Rlit.2	Retell stories, including key details, and demonstrate understanding of their central message or lesson.
258	**Think and Respond:** Talk About It	CA CC.1.Rlit.1	Ask and answer questions about key details in a text.
		CA CC.1.Rlit.2	Retell stories, including key details, and demonstrate understanding of their central message or lesson.
		CA CC.1.Rlit.3	Describe characters, settings, and major events in a story, using key details.
		CA CC.1.SL.6	Produce complete sentences when appropriate to task and situation. (See grade 1 Language standards 1 and 3 for specific expectations.)
	Think and Respond: Write About It	CA CC.1.W.8	With guidance and support from adults, recall information from experiences or gather information from provided sources to answer a question.
		CA CC.1.L.6	Use words and phrases acquired through conversations, reading and being read to, and responding to texts, including using frequently occurring conjunctions to signal simple relationships (e.g., *because*).
259	**Reread and Retell:** Identify Problem and Solution	CA CC.1.Rlit.2	Retell stories, including key details, and demonstrate understanding of their central message or lesson.
		CA CC.1.W.8	With guidance and support from adults, recall information from experiences or gather information from provided sources to answer a question.
		CA CC.1.SL.4	Describe people, places, things, and events with relevant details, expressing ideas and feelings clearly.
260	**Word Work:** Prefixes		Determine or clarify the meaning of unknown and multiple-meaning words and phrases based on *grade 1 reading and content*, choosing flexibly from an array of strategies.
		CA CC.1.L.4.b	Use frequently occurring affixes as a clue to the meaning of a word.
261–265	**Selection 2:** How-To Article How to Make a Compass	CA CC.1.Rinf.10	With prompting and support, read informational texts appropriately complex for grade 1.
266	**Respond and Extend:** Compare Genres	CA CC.1.Rlit.5	Explain major differences between books that tell stories and books that give information, drawing on a wide reading of a range of text types.
		CA CC.1.SL.1	Participate in collaborative conversations with diverse partners about *grade 1 topics and texts* with peers and adults in small and larger groups.
		CA CC.1.SL.4	Describe people, places, things, and events with relevant details, expressing ideas and feelings clearly.
267	**Grammar and Spelling:** Prepositions		Demonstrate command of the conventions of standard English grammar and usage when writing or speaking.
		CA CC.1.L.1.i	Use frequently occurring prepositions (e.g., *during, beyond, toward*).

SE Pages	Lesson	Code	Standard
268–269	**Writing Project:** Write a Literary Response	CA CC.1.W.1	Write opinion pieces in which they introduce the topic or name the book they are writing about, state an opinion, supply a reason for the opinion, and provide some sense of closure.
		CA CC.1.W.5	With guidance and support from adults, focus on a topic, respond to questions and suggestions from peers, and add details to strengthen writing as needed.
		CA CC.1.SL.1	Participate in collaborative conversations with diverse partners about *grade 1 topics and texts* with peers and adults in small and larger groups.
		CA CC.1.SL.4	Describe people, places, things, and events with relevant details, expressing ideas and feelings clearly.
			Demonstrate command of the conventions of standard English grammar and usage when writing or speaking.
		CA CC.1.L.1.i	Use frequently occurring prepositions (e.g., *during, beyond, toward*).
		CA CC.1.L.1.j	Produce and expand complete simple and compound declarative, interrogative, imperative, and exclamatory sentences in response to prompts.
			Demonstrate command of the conventions of standard English capitalization, punctuation, and spelling when writing.
		CA CC.1.L.2.d	Use conventional spelling for words with common spelling patterns and for frequently occurring irregular words.
		CA CC.1.L.2.e	Spell untaught words phonetically, drawing on phonemic awareness and spelling conventions.
270–271	**Unit Wrap-Up:** Share Your Ideas	CA CC.1.W.8	With guidance and support from adults, recall information from experiences or gather information from provided sources to answer a question.
			Participate in collaborative conversations with diverse partners about *grade 1 topics and texts* with peers and adults in small and larger groups.
		CA CC.1.SL.1.a	Follow agreed-upon rules for discussions (e.g., listening to others with care, speaking one at a time about the topics and texts under discussion).
		CA CC.1.SL.1.c	Ask questions to clear up any confusion about the topics and texts under discussion.
		CA CC.1.SL.2	Ask and answer questions about key details in a text read aloud or information presented orally or through other media.
		CA CC.1.SL.2.a	**Give, restate, and follow simple two-step directions. CA**
		CA CC.1.SL.4	Describe people, places, things, and events with relevant details, expressing ideas and feelings clearly.
		CA CC.1.SL.5	Add drawings or other visual displays to descriptions when appropriate to clarify ideas, thoughts, and feelings.
		CA CC.1.L.6	Use words and phrases acquired through conversations, reading and being read to, and responding to texts, including using frequently occurring conjunctions to signal simple relationships (e.g., *because*).